Math
Brainstorms

by
Becky Daniel

illustrated by Nancee McClure

Cover by Nancee McClure

Good Apple, Inc.
1204 Buchanan St., Box 299
Carthage, IL 62321-0299

Copyright © Good Apple, Inc., 1990

ISBN No. 0-86653-565-9

Printing No. 987654

Good Apple, Inc.
1204 Buchanan St., Box 299
Carthage, IL 62321-0299

SE
AFJ 9826

Table of Contents

GA1170

To the Teacher

Math Brainstorms is designed to teach early grade students figural reasoning, visual discrimination skills and promote inductive reasoning. Most elementary math lessons involve a great deal of rote learning, and one of the problems facing educators is how to teach our children to think analytically. Children often memorize the basic math facts but seldom practice relational techniques. Although memorizing math facts is an important skill, thinking skills are also needed.

To prepare your students to use the work sheets found herein, it is important to realize that reading the directions may be difficult or impossible for beginning readers. It is therefore suggested that the directions be given in small groups and the examples carefully explained before children are sent back to their desks to do independent seatwork.

Math Brainstorms includes activities to introduce estimating, common attributes, geometry, coordinates, optical illusions and fractions. The fun-filled puzzles and activities are guaranteed to make mathematics an enjoyable learning experience for all.

Bonus activities are found on many pages. These activities are usually more difficult and should not be a requirement. Use the bonus activities for extra credit. Students that complete these should receive special recognition. A class competition could involve keeping track of how many bonus activities are completed by each student and rewarding those that complete a given number. Awards are found on pages 75 and 76 and a special award certificate for bonus activities is included.

GA11

Guesstamation

Estimating means taking a guess at the number of something. *Guesstamation* is a made-up word for guessing numbers. Learning to guesstamate is an important skill. Before you count things, take a guess at how many there will be. Or before you work a math problem, guess what the answer will be. Soon you will develop your power of guesstamation.

Guess how many pieces of gum there are in the gum ball machine below. Write your guess here. _____

Count the pieces of gum and see how close your guesstamation was to the total amount. Did you guess too high or too low? _____

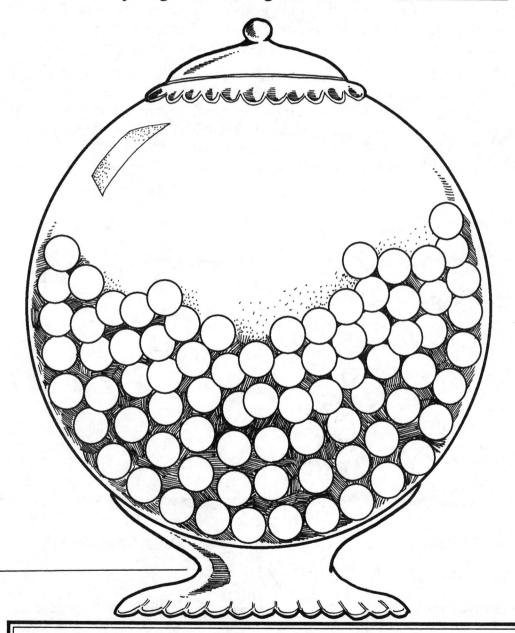

me _____

Bonus: Guess how many days there are until your birthday. Use a calendar and count to see how close your guesstamation was.

GA1170

More Guesstamation

Guess how many marbles there are in each of the four bags below. Then count and write the actual number. Find the difference between your guesstamation and the number of marbles in each bag. Do you usually guess high or low?

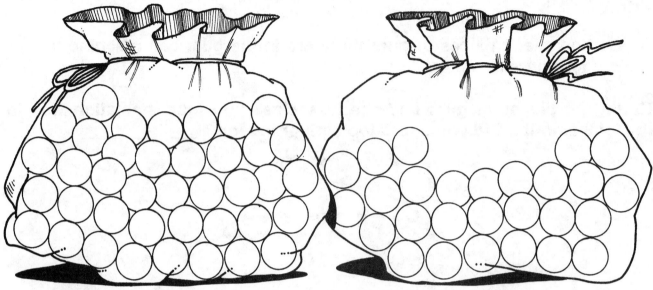

1. Guesstamation _____

   Total _____

   Difference _____

2. Guesstamation _____

   Total _____

   Difference _____

3. Guesstamation _____

   Total _____

   Difference _____

4. Guesstamation _____

   Total _____

   Difference _____

Bonus: Guess the total number of marbles in all four bags. Add the totals together to find the sum. How close was your guesstamation?

GA11

Go Ahead, Take a Guess

Guesstamate the answer for each question below. Then go outside to count and record the actual numbers. Write the difference between each guesstamation and answer.

Name _____

1. How many cars in the school parking lot?
   Guesstamation _____
   Total _____
   Difference _____

2. How many trees on the school grounds?
   Guesstamation _____
   Total _____
   Difference _____

3. How many windows in the school office?
   Guesstamation _____
   Total _____
   Difference _____

4. In inches, how tall is the classroom door?
   Guesstamation _____
   Total _____
   Difference _____

5. How many doors in the whole school?
   Guesstamation _____
   Total _____
   Difference _____

6. How many trash cans on the school grounds?
   Guesstamation _____
   Total _____
   Difference _____

7. How many drinking fountains at your school?
   Guesstamation _____
   Total _____
   Difference _____

8. How many of the seven questions above will you guess exactly right?
   Guesstamation _____
   Total _____
   Difference _____

Bonus: Guess how tall the principal is. Ask him/her how tall he/she is to find out how close you were.

GA1170

The Price Is Right

Before you add the bill for each bag of candy below, guesstamate each bill. Write your guesstamations. Next find the sum for each bag of candy. Record the difference between your guesstamation and each total.

 5¢  30¢  10¢ 2¢ each

1.
Guesstamation _____

Total _____

Difference _____

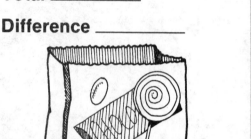

4.
Guesstamation _____

Total _____

Difference _____

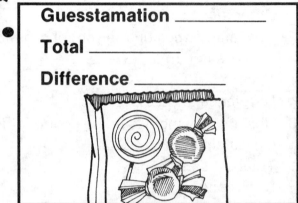

2.
Guesstamation _____

Total _____

Difference _____

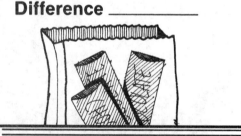

5.
Guesstamation _____

Total _____

Difference _____

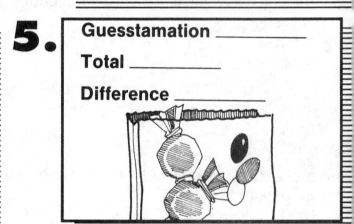

3.
Guesstamation _____

Total _____

Difference _____

6.
Guesstamation _____

Total _____

Difference _____

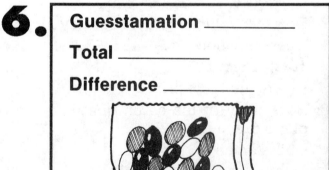

Bonus: Guesstamate the total of all six bags of candy. Write your guesstamation here. _____ Then add the actual totals to find the sum. What was the difference between your guess and the total? _____

4

Number Scavenger Hunt

Numbers are everywhere! Big numbers, little numbers, all help us keep track of the many things we must know. Today we are going to have a race to find numbers. How many of the numbers indicated below will you be able to find? Guesstamate. Write your guess here. _____ As you find each number, check it off and indicate where you found it on the line. You may not use the same source for more than one number on your list. If you find the number 31 in your reading book, you may not use your reading book as the source for another number. Ready? Set. Go!

1. 9 _____

2. 31 _____

3. any number between 50 and 60 _____

4. any three-digit number with the same number repeated (example: 888) _____

5. a number that looks like a letter _____

6. a two-digit number that can be read upside down (example: 66 = 99) _____

7. any number over 1000 _____

8. your lucky number printed somewhere _____

9. the largest number you can find _____

10. a digit more than one-inch high _____

Name _____

Bonus: Can you find a number written in Roman numerals?

GA1170

Favorite Color Graph

Graphs are pictorial charts that compare amounts of things. The graph below shows eight children's favorite colors. Color the graph as indicated. Then use the circle graph of favorite colors to answer each question below.

Name _____

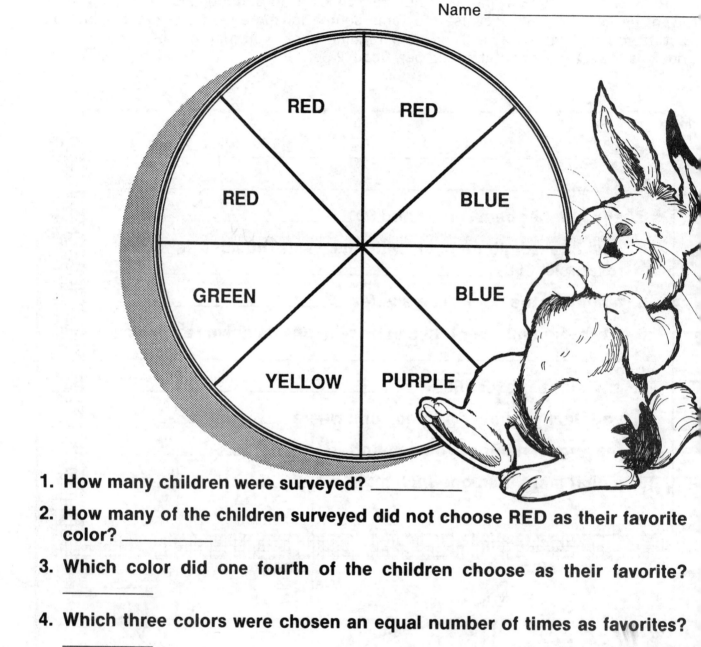

1. **How many children were surveyed?** _____

2. **How many of the children surveyed did not choose RED as their favorite color?** _____

3. **Which color did one fourth of the children choose as their favorite?** _____

4. **Which three colors were chosen an equal number of times as favorites?** _____

5. **What fractional part of the children surveyed chose RED as their favorite color?** _____

6. **What fractional part of the children surveyed chose RED or BLUE as their favorite color?** _____

Bonus: Survey twelve children to find out what their favorite colors are and create your own circle graph.

GA11

The Eyes Have It!

Survey twelve children to find out what colors their eyes are. Record the eye colors on a separate sheet of paper. Then complete the eye color bar graph below.

ne _____

10				
9				
8				
7				
6				
5				
4				
3				
2				
1				
	BLUE	GREEN	BROWN	HAZEL

Bonus: Using the information on your bar graph, create an eye color circle graph.

GA1170

Flight Graph

Make a paper airplane. Go outside with your airplane and a yardstick. Fly your plane ten times, recording each time how far it traveled to the nearest yard. Use the graph below to record each flight distance.

Name _____

1.									
2.									
3.									
4.									
5.									
6.									
7.									
8.									
9.									
10.									
Yards	1	2	4	5	6	7	8	9	10

Bonus: Find the average number of yards your plane traveled.

8

Pie Graph

Survey twelve friends to find out which of the pies listed below are their favorites. They must choose one favorite. Record the twelve answers and then use the pie graph found below to show the information. You will have to label the pie sections appropriately. Remember to show all those who choose peach pie together on the graph, apple selections together, etc.

PEACH   APPLE   PUMPKIN   BERRY   LEMON

Name _____

Bonus: Create a bar graph showing the favorite pie information above.

GA1170

Using Your Pie Graph

Using the pie graph on the previous page, answer each question below.

1. **What fractional part of the friends you surveyed liked peach pie best?** _____

2. **What fractional part of the friends you surveyed liked apple pie best?** _____

3. **What fractional part of the friends you surveyed liked pumpkin pie best?** _____

4. **What fractional part of the friends you surveyed liked berry pie best?** _____

5. **What fractional part of the friends you surveyed liked lemon pie best?** _____

6. **Do any two pie favorites equal more than one half of those surveyed? Which two?** _____

7. **What is the most popular pie flavor?** _____

8. **What is the least popular pie flavor?** _____

Name _____

Bonus: Using a cake-shaped graph, survey ten friends and record their favorite cake flavors.

Picture That!

Study the shape of the four sections in the square below. Then using the letter in each shape, carefully answer each question.

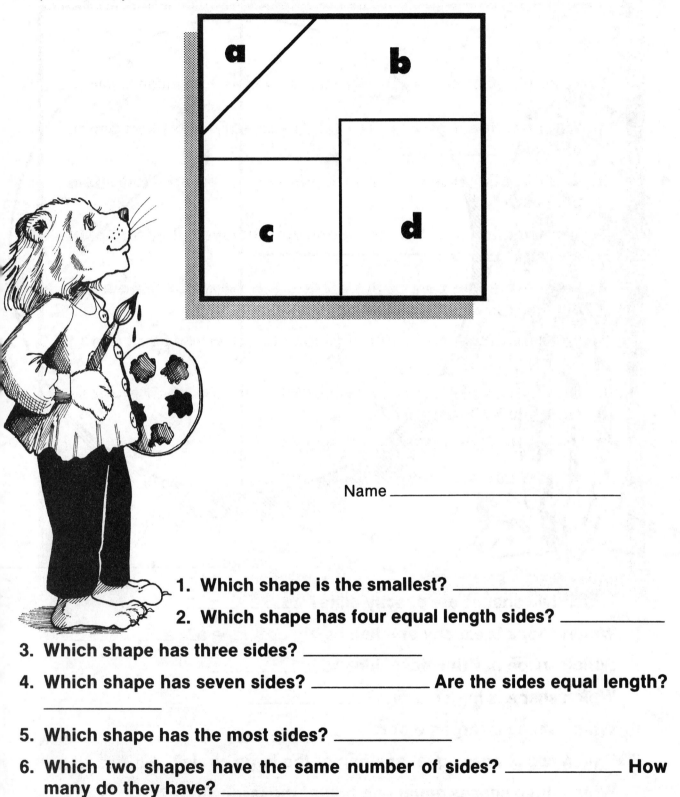

Name _____

1. **Which shape is the smallest?** _____

2. **Which shape has four equal length sides?** _____

3. **Which shape has three sides?** _____

4. **Which shape has seven sides?** _____ **Are the sides equal length?**
_____

5. **Which shape has the most sides?** _____

6. **Which two shapes have the same number of sides?** _____ **How many do they have?** _____

Bonus: About what fractional part of C is A?

 GA1170

Circle Designs

Study the shapes within the circle below. Using the letter inside each shape, carefully answer each question.

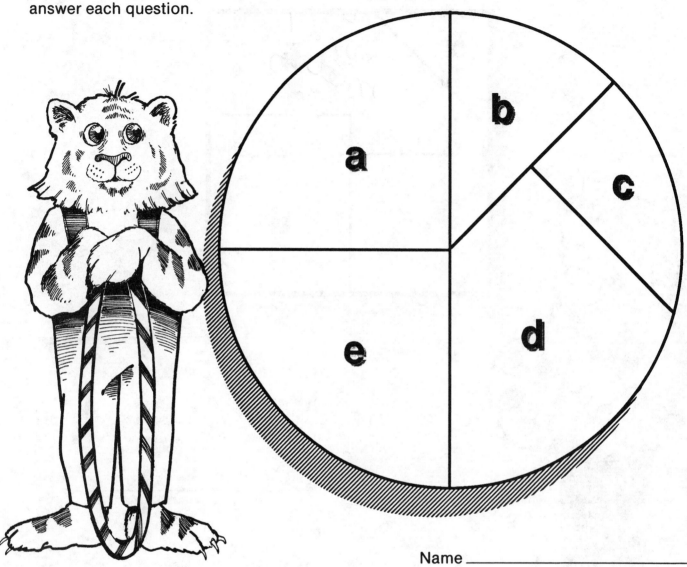

Name _____

1. **Which two shapes are exactly alike?** _____

2. **Which shape is exactly one half as big as shape a?** _____

3. **Which shape has the most sides?** _____

4. **Which shape is larger, a or c?** _____

5. **Which shape is larger, e or c?** _____

6. **Which two shapes equal one half of the large circle?** _____

7. **Which three shapes equal one half of the large circle?** _____

Bonus: Which shape represents the fractional part ⅛ of the large circle?

12

Building Shapes

Using the letters inside the four shapes, carefully answer each question below.

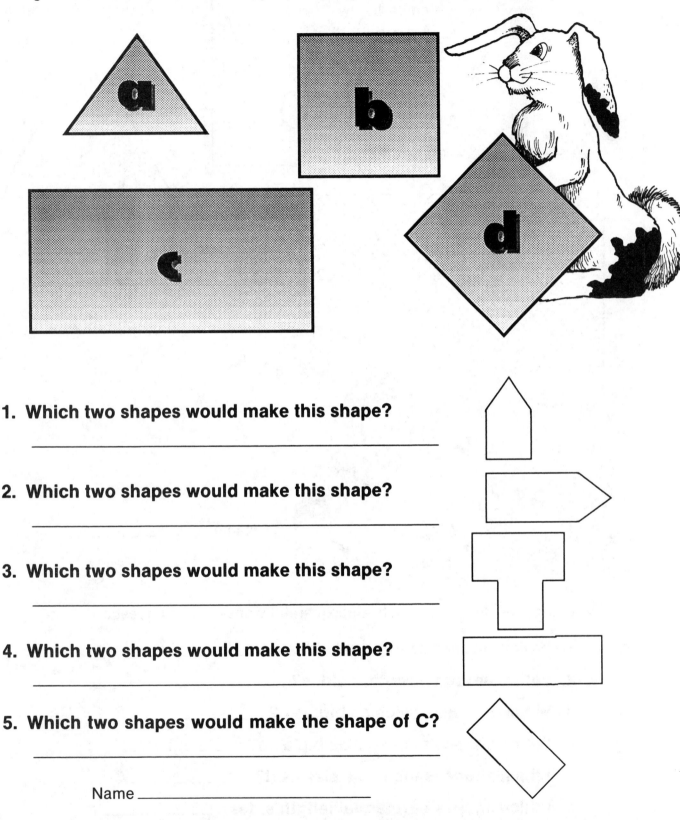

1. **Which two shapes would make this shape?**

   _____

2. **Which two shapes would make this shape?**

   _____

3. **Which two shapes would make this shape?**

   _____

4. **Which two shapes would make this shape?**

   _____

5. **Which two shapes would make the shape of C?**

   _____

   Name _____

Bonus: Using all four shapes, each as many times as you wish, draw and color a design.

13

GA1170

Study the Shapes

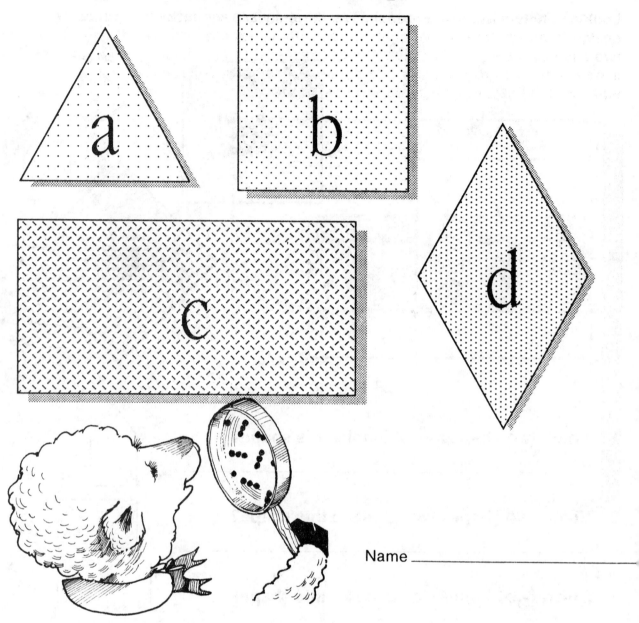

Name _____

Using the letter inside each shape, carefully answer each question.

1. **Which figure has unequal sides?** _____

2. **Which figures have four sides?** _____

3. **Which shape is twice as big as b?** _____

4. **Which shapes are twice as big as a?** _____

5. **Which shape is the same size as d?** _____

6. **Which shapes have equal length sides?** _____

> **Bonus:** Write the word for each shape.

14

Two Are Out!

Look carefully at the shape below. The large square has four small squares within. The design is drawn with twelve lines. If you remove exactly two lines, you will be left with two squares instead of four. Redraw the design with only ten equal length lines in such a way that you have exactly two squares. Example: This design was drawn with ten equal length lines, but it is three squares, not two:

Name _____

Bonus: Can you draw six triangles using only thirteen lines?

Circle One!

Circle the design in each row that is exactly like the first design.

Example:

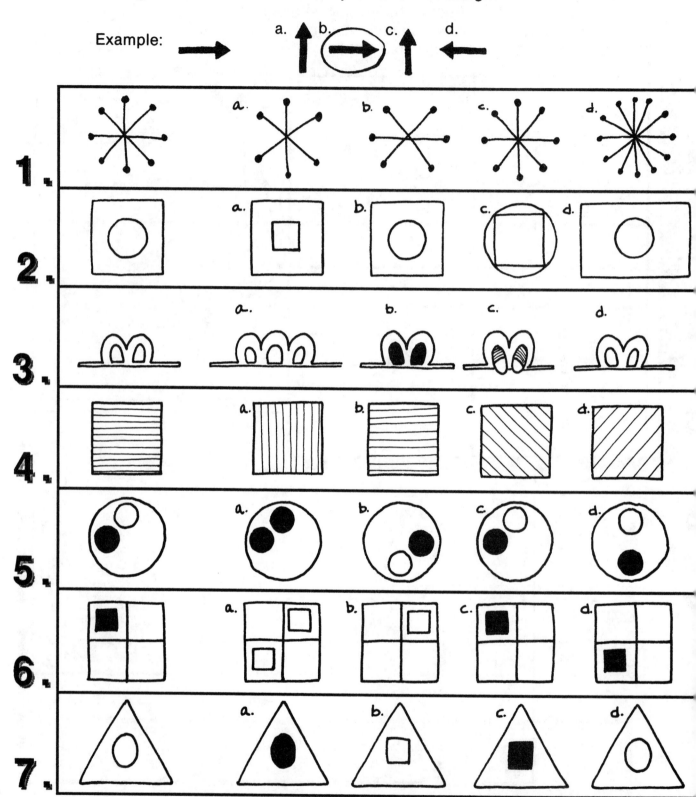

Bonus: Circle the two matching designs below.

16

Twin Designs

Circle the two designs in each row that are exactly the same.

Example: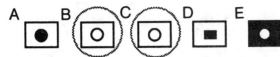

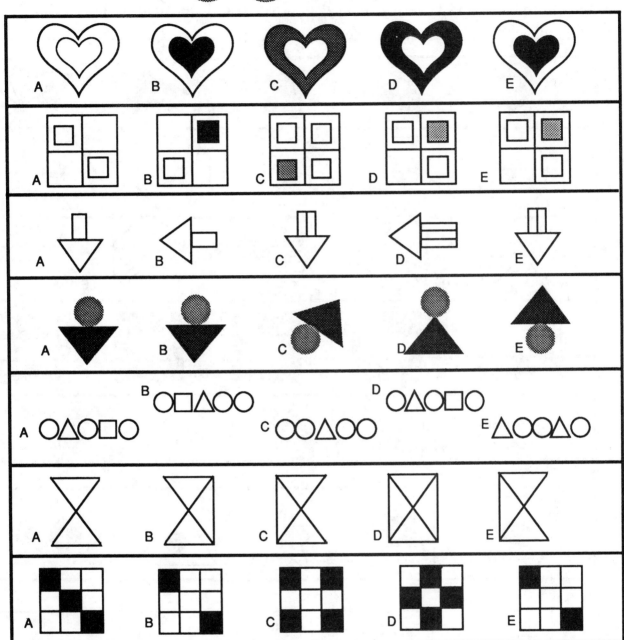

Name _____

Bonus: Circle the two matching designs below.

GA1170

Cross Out!

Cross out the design that doesn't belong in each row.

Example:

The design that doesn't have a star in it is crossed out because all the designs have a star except that one.

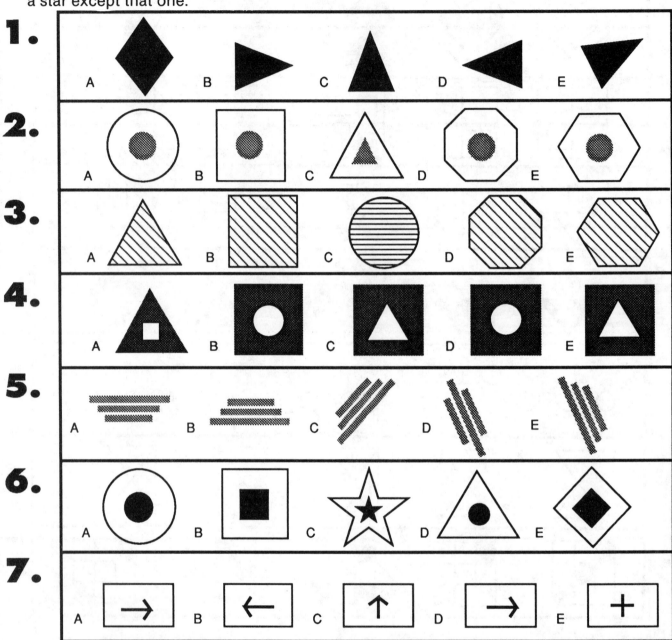

1.
A   B   C   D   E

2.
A   B   C   D   E

3.
A   B   C   D   E

4.
A   B   C   D   E

5.
A   B   C   D   E

6.
A   B   C   D   E

7.
A   B   C   D   E

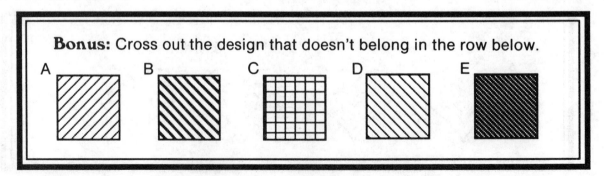

Bonus: Cross out the design that doesn't belong in the row below.

A   B   C   D   E

GA117

What's Next?

Circle the design that should come next in each row.   Name _____

Example:

The first arrow is circled because the three arrows on the left are moving in a circle clockwise.

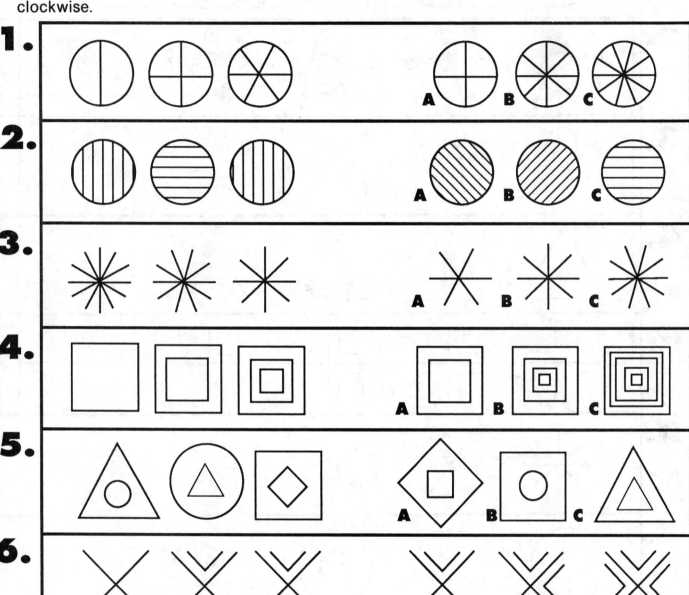

Bonus: Draw the design that should follow those below.

19   GA1170

Draw What's Next

Draw the design that you think should come next in each row below.

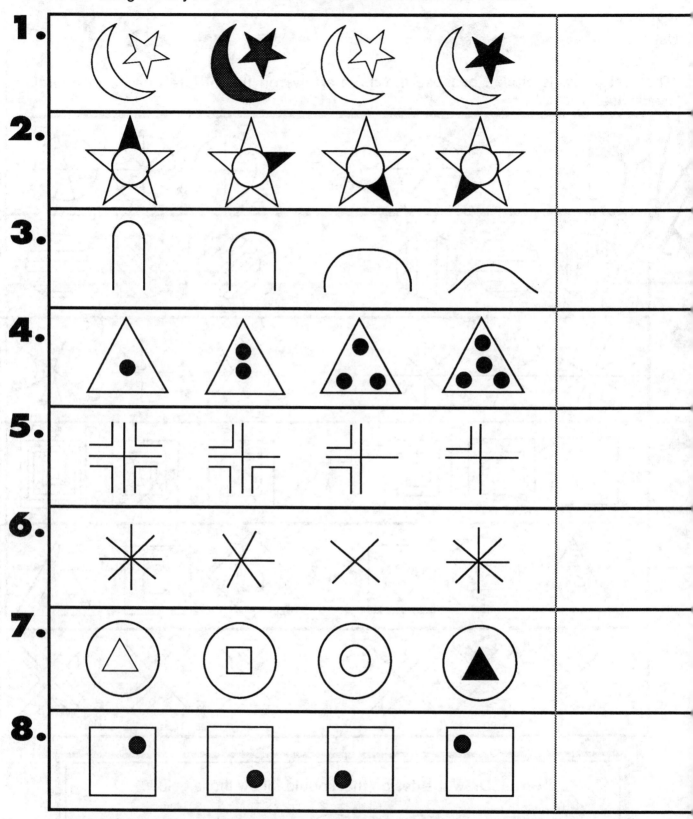

1.

2.

3.

4.

5.

6.

7.

8.

Bonus: Draw a series of five designs with a special pattern. See if a friend can determine your pattern.

20

GA117

Shapes

Use the shapes to complete each box below.

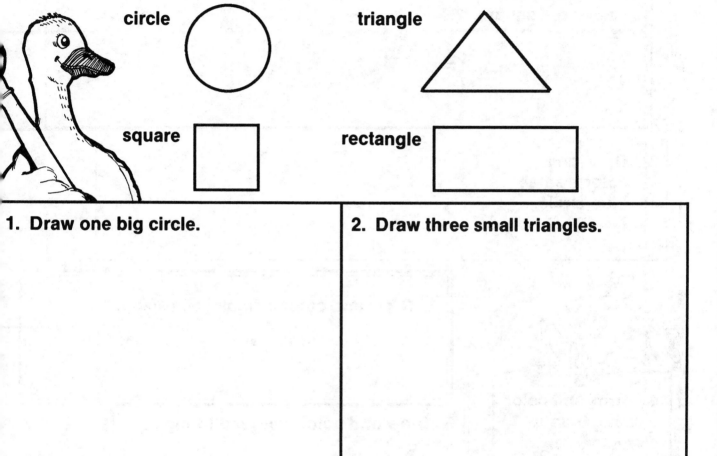

circle

triangle

square

rectangle

1. Draw one big circle.	**2. Draw three small triangles.**
3. Draw four big squares.	**4. Draw five small rectangles.**

Bonus: Draw a big circle with a small square inside it.

GA1170

Draw and Color

Follow the directions in each box below.

1. **Draw and color a big red square.**

2. **Draw and color a small blue circle.**

3. **Draw and color a small yellow square.**

4. **Draw and color a big blue rectangle.**

5. **Draw and color a big red triangle.**

6. **Draw and color a small yellow circle.**

Bonus: Draw a big blue circle with a small yellow circle inside it.

GA11

Logic Blocks

Color the twenty-four logic blocks below. Use this page with the attribute lessons on pages 24-26.

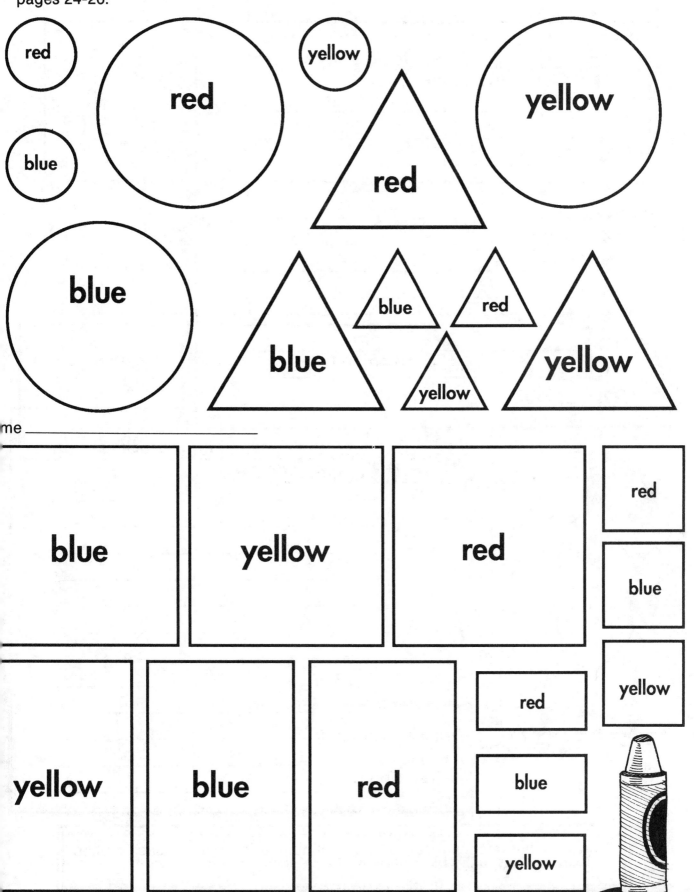

me _____

23

GA1170

Just the Right Size

To answer the questions below, use the logic blocks on page 23.

1. How many large-shaped logic blocks are on page 23? List them here.

1. _____
2. _____
3. _____
4. _____
5. _____
6. _____
7. _____
8. _____
9. _____
10. _____
11. _____
12. _____

2. How many small-shaped logic blocks are on page 23? List them here.

1. _____
2. _____
3. _____
4. _____
5. _____
6. _____
7. _____
8. _____
9. _____
10. _____
11. _____
12. _____

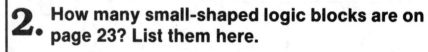

Bonus: What fractional part of the total number of logic blocks on page 23 are small? Big?

GA1

Color, Please!

To answer the questions below, use the logic blocks on page 23.

1. **How many logic blocks on page 23 are the same color as the small red circle?**

List them here.

1. _____
2. _____
3. _____
4. _____
5. _____
6. _____
7. _____

2. **How many logic blocks on page 23 are the same color as the big blue circle?**

List them here.

1. _____
2. _____
3. _____
4. _____
5. _____
6. _____
7. _____

Name _____

Bonus: What fractional part of the logic blocks on page 23 are red? Yellow? Blue?

GA1170

Shape Up!

To answer the questions below, use the logic blocks on page 23.

1. **How many logic blocks on page 23 are the same shape as the small blue square?**

   List them here.

   1. _____
   2. _____
   3. _____
   4. _____
   5. _____

2. **How many logic blocks on page 23 are the same shape as the big red circle?**

   List them here.

   1. _____
   2. _____
   3. _____
   4. _____
   5. _____

3. **How many logic blocks on page 23 are the same shape as the small blue triangle?**

   List them here.

   1. _____
   2. _____
   3. _____
   4. _____
   5. _____

Bonus: What fractional part of the logic blocks on page 23 are triangles? Circles? Rectangles? Squares?

Common Attribute

The logic blocks that you have been working with have three attributes—size, color and shape. Example: The big blue square and the big red circle have one common attribute—size. The small red triangle and the big red square have one common attribute—color. To complete this page, you must list the common attribute for each pair of logic blocks in the boxes below. Is it size, color or shape?

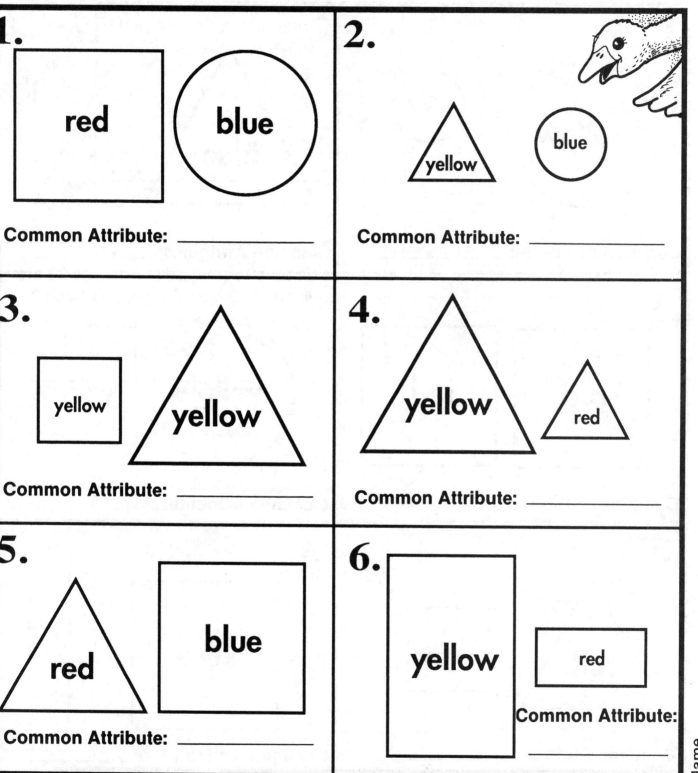

1.

red   blue

Common Attribute: _____

2.

yellow   blue

Common Attribute: _____

3.

yellow   yellow

Common Attribute: _____

4.

yellow   red

Common Attribute: _____

5.

red   blue

Common Attribute: _____

6.

yellow   red

Common Attribute: _____

Name _____

Bonus: Draw two logic blocks that have no common attributes.

GA1170

Counting Attributes

Remember the logic block attributes are size, color and shape. Count the number of common attributes that each pair of logic blocks has. Example: The small red circle and the large red circle have two common attributes—color and shape.

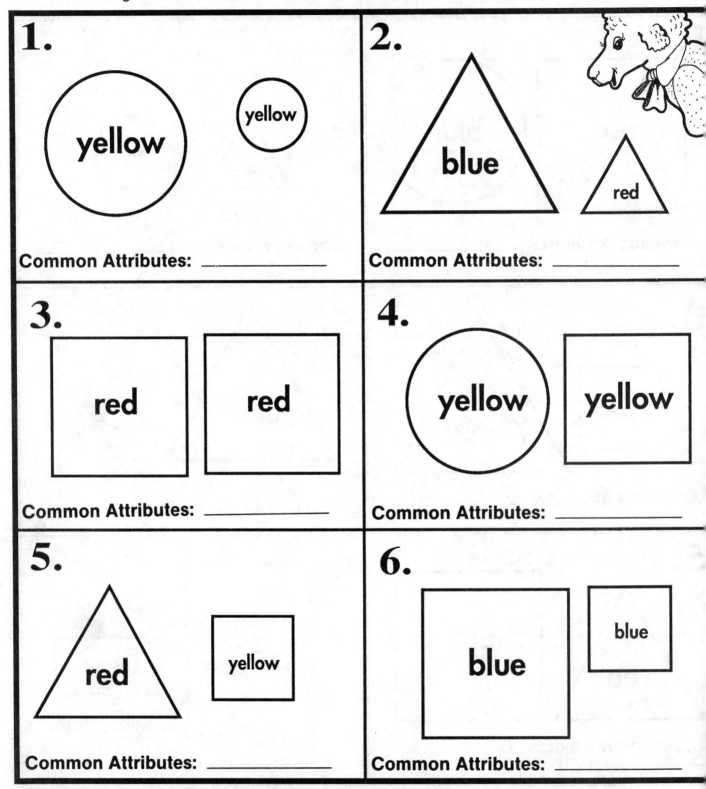

1.

yellow   yellow

Common Attributes: _____

2.

blue   red

Common Attributes: _____

3.

red   red

Common Attributes: _____

4.

yellow   yellow

Common Attributes: _____

5.

red   yellow

Common Attributes: _____

6.

blue   blue

Common Attributes: _____

Bonus: Draw three logic blocks that have one common attribute.

28

GA

Name the Way

In each box below list the attribute that the logic block pair has in common—size, color or shape.

1.

blue   red

_____

2.

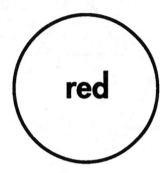

red   blue

_____

3.

red   blue

_____

4.

red   red

_____

5.

yellow   blue

_____

6.

red   yellow

_____

Bonus: Draw two attribute blocks that have three common attributes.

29   GA1170

You Decide

Color the logic block pairs so that each set has only one common attribute. Example: If the logic blocks are already the same shape or the same size, color them different colors. If the logic blocks are a different size and shape, then color them the same color.

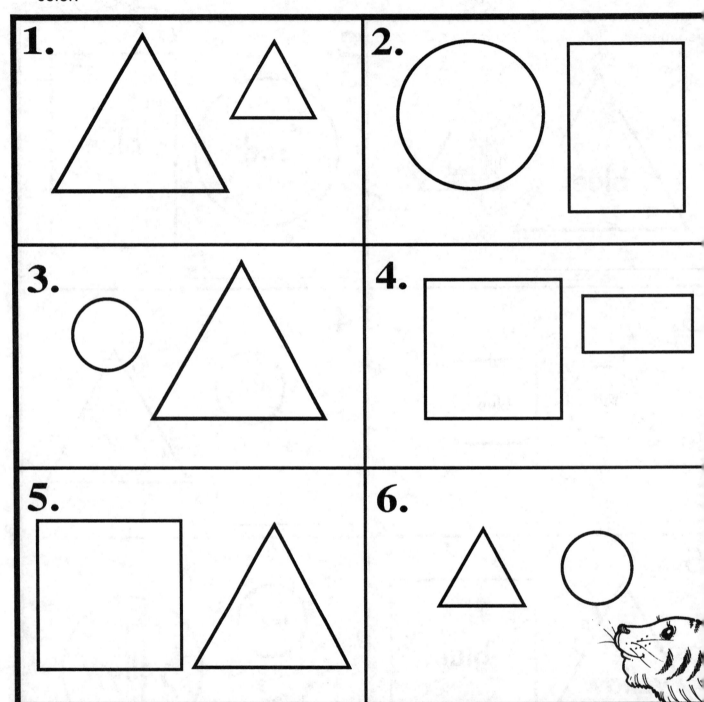

1.

2.

3.

4.

5.

6.

Bonus: Draw a string of six logic blocks so that each block has one common attribute with the next block. You may not repeat the use of any one block. Example: If you use the big blue triangle, you may not use a big blue triangle in your string of logic blocks again.

GA11

Geograms Set I

Geograms is a made-up word for shapes cut from a square or rectangle. Carefully cut on the solid lines to create the five-piece Geograms Set I. You will need these geograms to complete pages 32-33.

After you cut the square into five geograms, see if you can put it back together in the shape of a square. Can you make a rectangle? Diamond?

Name _____

GA1170

Geogram Design #1

Using only three pieces of Geograms Set I on page 31, can you create this shape?

Bonus: Using all five pieces of the geograms on page 31, can you make this shape? ➡️

GA

Geogram Design #2

Using three pieces of Geograms Set I on page 31, can you create this shape?

Bonus: Using four of the five pieces of the geograms on page 31, can you create this shape?

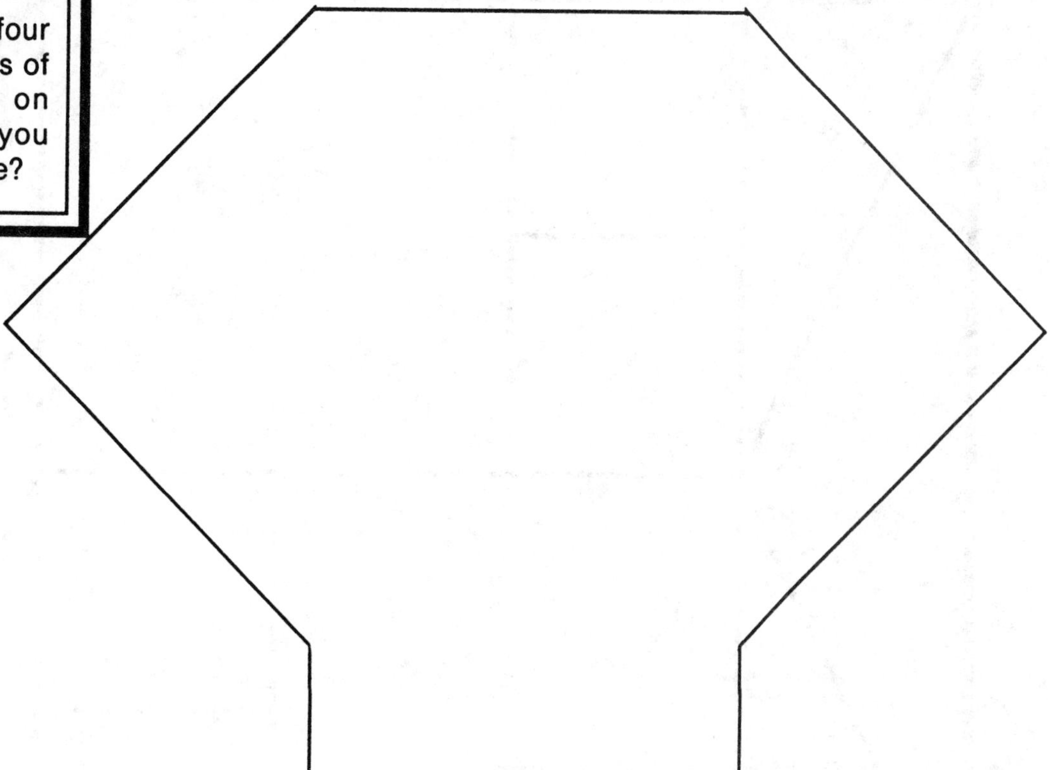

Name _____

GA1170

Geograms Set II

Geograms are twelve shapes cut from a large rectangle. Carefully cut along the solid lines to create your second set of geograms.

Can you create a square with nine of the twelve pieces?

Name _____

GA1

Geogram Design #3

Using ten of the twelve geograms cut from a rectangle on page 34, can you create this shape?

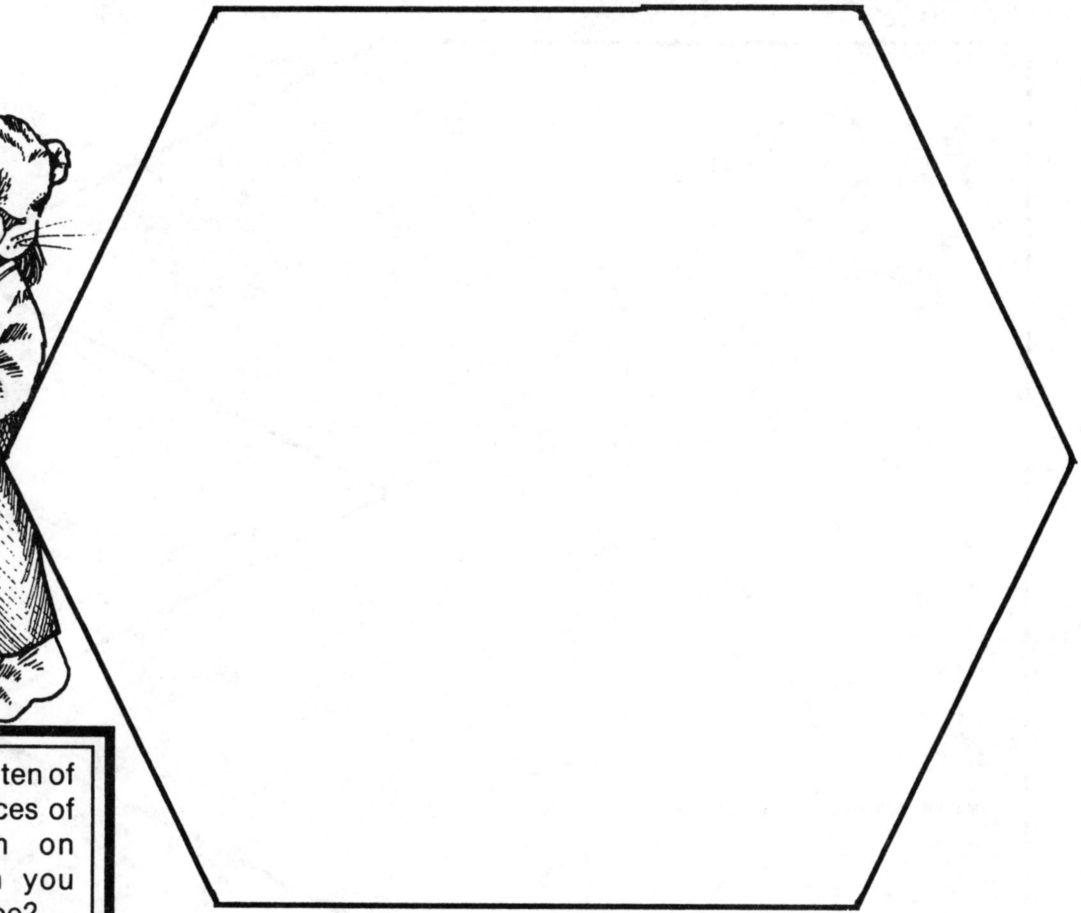

Bonus: Using ten of the twelve pieces of the geogram on page 34, can you make this shape? →

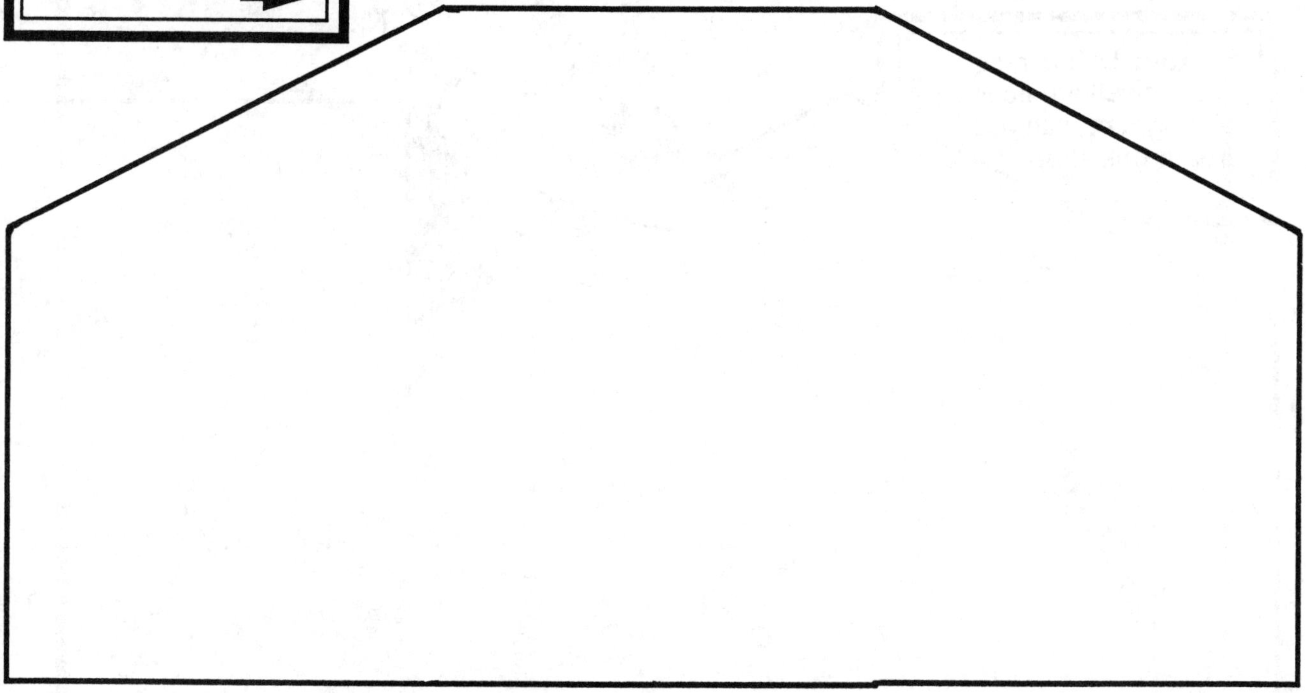

Name _____

GA1170

Geogram Design #4

Using only eleven of the twelve pieces of Geograms Set II on page 34, can you create this shape?

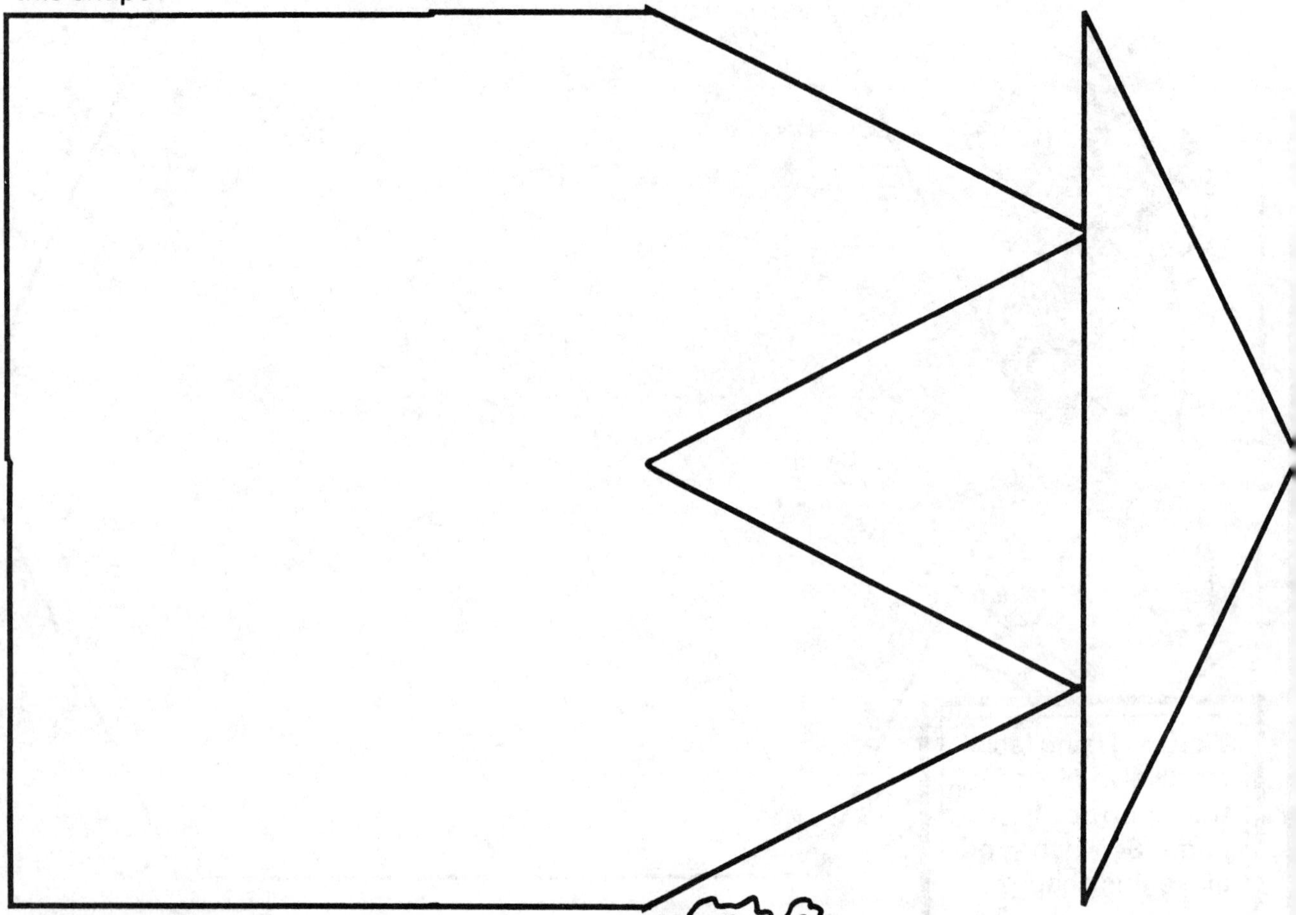

Name _____

Bonus: Using nine of the twelve pieces of geograms, can you create this shape?

36

Lakeview Homes

Use the map and key below to answer each question. Your answers will be rounded off to the nearest one hundred yards. Children must begin each journey from their front doors.

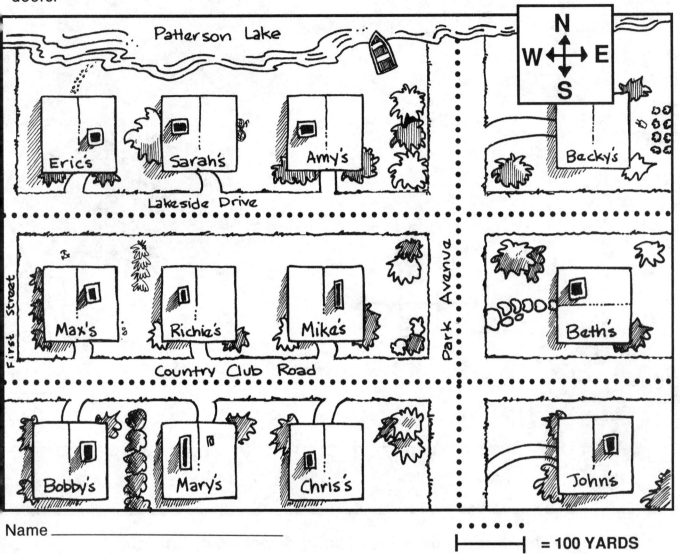

Name _____   ├———┤ = 100 YARDS

1. **How far does John have to walk to get to the lake's edge?** _____

2. **Which three children could go out their back doors and see the lake?**

   _____

3. **How far is the lake from Bobby's house?** _____

4. **How far is it from Beth's house to Sarah's house?** _____

5. **How much farther from the lake does Max live than Becky?** _____

> **Bonus:** Chris rides his bike down Country Club Road to First Street and straight north to the lake, because Park Avenue doesn't have a bike trail. How far does he ride his bike when he goes to the lake?

Hidden Lunch Money

Every day for one week, John's father gave him a note telling him where he had hid John's lunch money. Use the map of John's room to figure out where John should look for his lunch money.

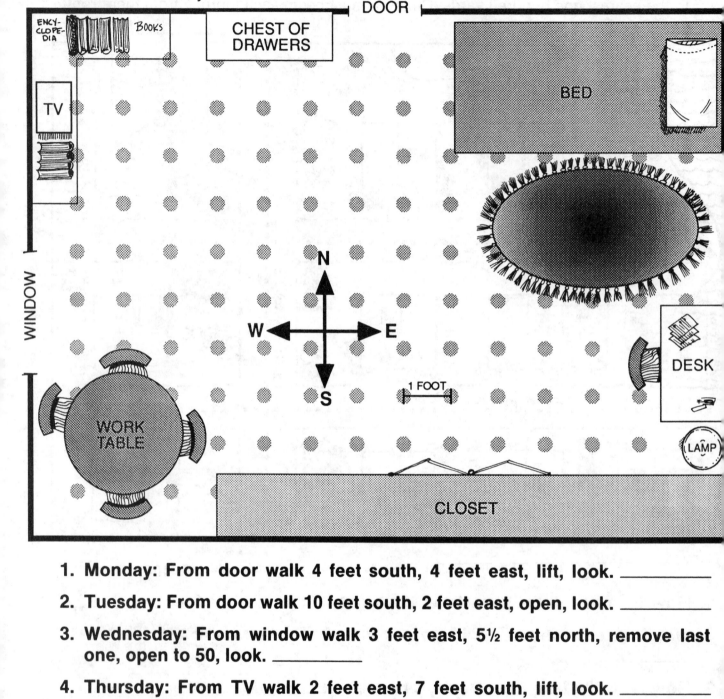

1. **Monday: From door walk 4 feet south, 4 feet east, lift, look.** _____

2. **Tuesday: From door walk 10 feet south, 2 feet east, open, look.** _____

3. **Wednesday: From window walk 3 feet east, 5½ feet north, remove last one, open to 50, look.** _____

4. **Thursday: From TV walk 2 feet east, 7 feet south, lift, look.** _____

5. **Friday: From door walk 6 feet south, 2 feet west, 5 feet north, pull top, look.** _____

Name _____

Bonus: Pretend you have hidden something in John's bedroom. Write the directions for finding it.

GA117

Dry Caves Island

Pretend you and a friend have landed a canoe on Dry Caves Island at *. Use the map and key to answer each question below.

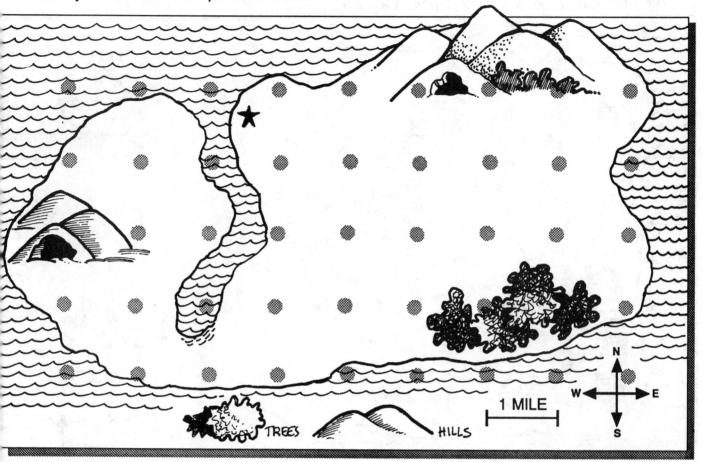

1. You want to reach the southern tip of the stream by canoe. How far will you have to paddle? _____

2. After reaching the southern tip of the stream, you and your friend decide to leave the canoe there and walk to get wood for a fire. How far will you have to walk? _____

3. After gathering wood, you decide to walk back to the cave on the west shore of the island. How far will you walk? _____

4. You and your friend build a fire and cook fish for dinner. You are going to sleep in the cave that night. How far from the cave will you have to walk in the morning to get to your canoe? _____

5. The next day you plan to paddle your canoe back up to where you landed yesterday. How far will you paddle? _____

6. From the landing spot, how far will you have to walk to find the entrance to the cave on the north shore? _____

Name _____

Bonus: Draw a map of an island. Put some of your favorite things on the map.

Treasure Island

You and your best friend find an old map drawn by pirates more than a hundred years ago. You are dropped by helicopter onto the island to search for the treasure chest. Use the map below and mark your path with a blue crayon. Then mark the spot where you think the treasure is hidden with a red X.

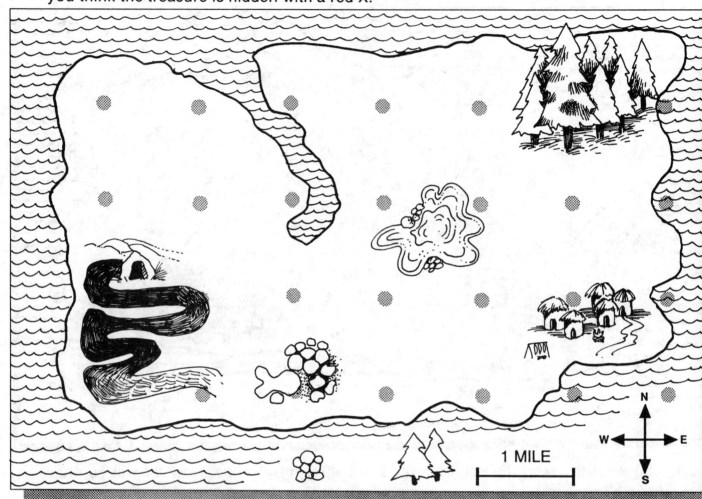

Big tree west 2 miles.

1 mile south.

Cross stream and walk 2 miles west.

1 mile south.

Follow tunnel south.

Go 1 mile east.

Look under fish-shaped rock.

Name _____

Bonus: Pretend you have hidden a treasure chest of gold on the island. Write the directions for finding your hidden treasure. See if your friend can follow your buried treasure directions.

GA11

Just Add a Plus Sign

Place a plus sign in each row of numbers below to make each number sentence true.
Example: 5 5 + 5 = 6 0

1. 3 2 1 = 3 3
2. 4 5 0 = 5 4
3. 1 2 3 = 1 5
4. 4 6 7 = 7 1
5. 9 2 1 = 9 3
6. 6 7 2 = 6 9
7. 7 8 2 = 8 0
8. 4 5 1 = 4 6
9. 2 9 0 = 9 2
10. 8 0 0 = 8 0

Name _____

Bonus: Add a plus sign and an equal sign to the row of numbers below to make a true number sentence.

5 4 2 4 7

GA1170

Plus or Minus?

Add a plus or a minus sign to each row of numbers to make the number sentence true.
Example: 4 5 – 3 = 4 2

1. 1 2 3 4 = 4 6

2. 3 3 3 3 = 0

3. 1 1 1 1 = 1 1 0

4. 5 5 5 5 = 5 6 0

5. 4 4 4 4 = 4 4 0

6. 2 2 2 2 = 4 4

7. 4 3 2 1 = 6 4

8. 9 8 7 6 = 2 2

Name _____

Bonus: Add a plus or minus sign and an equal sign to the row of numbers below to make a true number sentence.

6 6 6 6 6 7 2

GA117

Two Intersecting Sets

Look at the sets represented by the two intersecting circles.

A = The girls that live on Maple Street.

B = The boys and girls that live on Maple Street that are in Mrs. Lamb's class.

C = The boys that live on Maple Street.

Use the letters *ABC* to represent each set when answering the questions below.

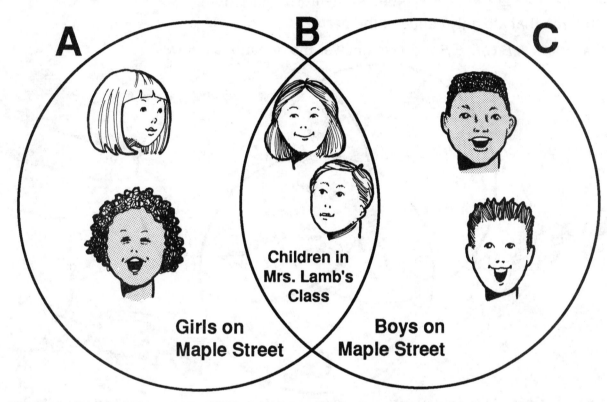

1. **Mark is in Mr. Roark's class and he lives on Maple Street. Which set does he belong to?** _____

2. **How many girls in Mrs. Lamb's class live on Maple Street?** _____

3. **If John belongs to set B, who is his teacher?** _____

4. **Are there any boys in Mrs. Lamb's class that live on Maple Street? _____ How many?** _____

5. **How many children live on Maple Street?** _____

6. **How many boys live on Maple Street?** _____

Name _____

Bonus: What fractional part of children living on Maple Street are in Mrs. Lamb's class?

    GA1170

Three Intersecting Sets

Below are three intersecting sets.

A = Children that ate ice cream at the party.

B = Children that ate ice cream and cake at the party.

C = Children that ate only cake at the party.

D = Children that ate ice cream and candy at the party.

E = Children that ate ice cream, cake and candy at the party.

F = Children that ate cake and candy at the party.

G = Children that ate only candy at the party.

Use the letters *A,B,C,D,E,F* and *G* to answer the questions below.

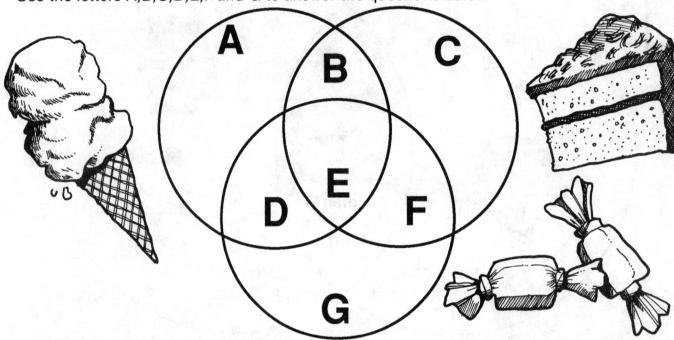

1. **If Mark had all three—cake, candy and ice cream—in which set does he belong?** _____

2. **If Mary loves sweet things but will not eat cold things, in which set does she belong?** _____

3. **If John is in set D, what did he eat at the party?** _____

4. **Crystal ate only ice cream at the party. In which set does she belong?** _____

5. **Beth ate ice cream and two slices of cake at the party. In which set does she belong?** _____

6. **Name the four sets that include ice cream.** _____

Name _____

Bonus: In which set would you belong, if you went to the party? _____

Optical Illusions

Looking is not always seeing. Think carefully before you answer each question below. Then use a ruler to check your answers.

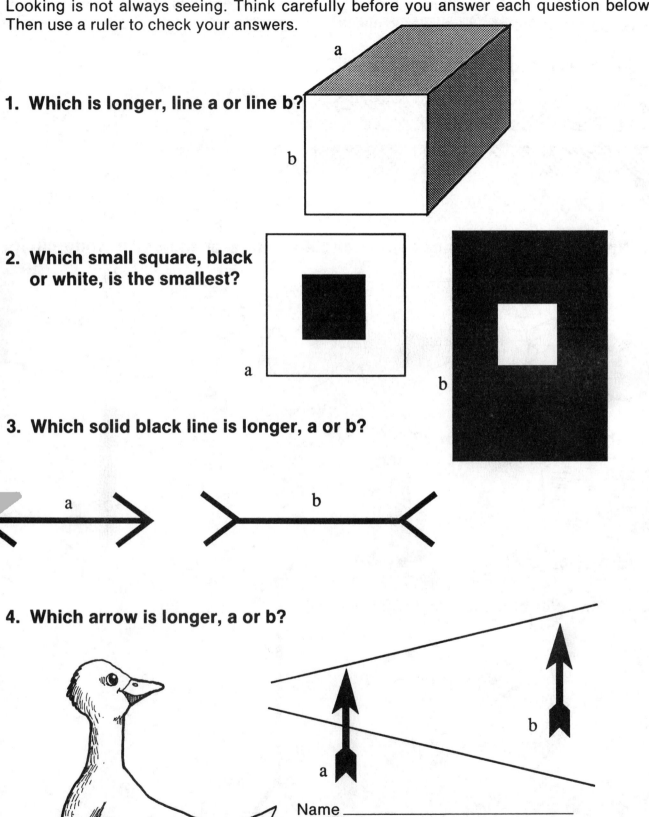

1. **Which is longer, line a or line b?**

2. **Which small square, black or white, is the smallest?**

3. **Which solid black line is longer, a or b?**

4. **Which arrow is longer, a or b?**

Name _____

Bonus: Using one of the concepts of an optical illusion on this page, draw your own optical illusion.

GA1170

More Optical Illusions

Did the first page of optical illusions teach you something about looking? Here are some more. Do not be fooled; use a ruler to check your answers.

1. Are lines a and b straight or curved?

2. Which is larger, the small white circle within a or the small white circle within b?

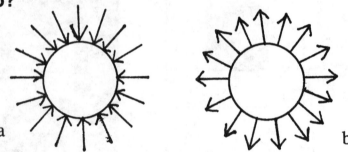

3. Which hat is taller, a or b?

4. Which solid black line is longer, a or b?

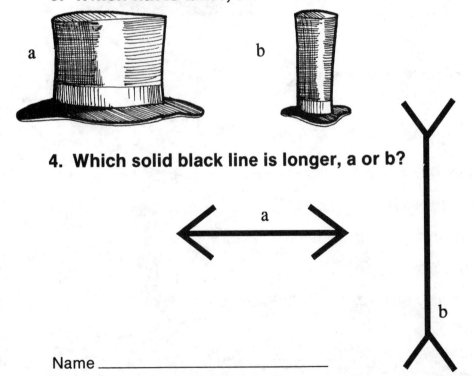

Name _____

Bonus: Using one of the illusion concepts on this page, create your own optical illusion.

GA1

Fruit Slices

To answer the questions, look carefully at the fruit slices below. One piece of banana equals ⅓, etc.

1. **What fractional part of a banana is one slice?** _____

2. **What fractional part of an apple is two slices?** _____

3. **What fractional part of an orange is three slices?** _____

4. **Which is a larger fractional part, ¼ or ⅕?** _____

5. **Are three slices of an orange more or less than ½ of the orange?**
_____

6. **Which is a larger fractional part, ⅓ or ¼?** _____

Name _____

Bonus: What fractional part of all the fruit is one piece of banana?

GA1170

Easy as Pie

To answer each question below, look carefully at the three pies. Each apple pie slice equals ¼ of the pie, etc.

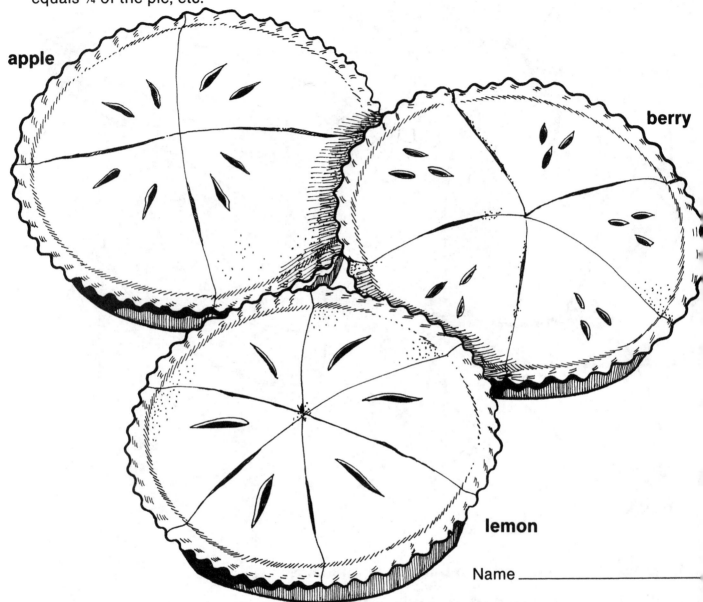

apple

berry

lemon

Name _____

1. **What fractional part of the apple pie is one piece?** _____

2. **What fractional part of the berry pie is one piece?** _____

3. **What fractional part of the lemon pie is one piece?** _____

4. **What fractional part of the lemon pie is three pieces?** _____

5. **How many pieces of pie are in ½ of the lemon pie?** _____

6. **How many pieces of pie are in ½ of the apple pie?** _____

Bonus: Two pieces of which pie would equal ⅓ of the total pie?

48

The Bobcats

To answer the questions below, look carefully at the children on the Bobcat baseball team. Remember: One team member equals ⅑ of the whole team.

1. What fractional part of the team is not wearing a cap? _____

2. What fractional part of the team is tossing a baseball? _____

3. What fractional part of the team is carrying a bat? _____

4. What fractional part of the team is wearing a mitt? _____

5. What fractional part of the team is girls? _____

6. What fractional part of the girls is wearing a catcher's mask? _____

Name _____

Bonus: Color the team caps and uniforms your favorite ball team's colors.

GA1170

Fraction Party

To answer the questions below, carefully look at the ten people at the party. One person equals ¹⁄₁₀ of the people at the party.

1. **What fractional part of the people are adults?** _____

2. **What fractional part of the people are male?** _____

3. **What fractional part of the people are wearing party hats?** _____

4. **What fractional part of the people have long hair?** _____

5. **What fractional part of the people are little boys?** _____

6. **What fractional part of the people at the party are wearing glasses?** _____

Name _____

Bonus: If both of the men leave the party, what fractional part of the people left will be little boys?

GA1

Line Design #1

Use a ruler to connect every point marked with the number 1 with every other point. The first few lines have been drawn to get you started.

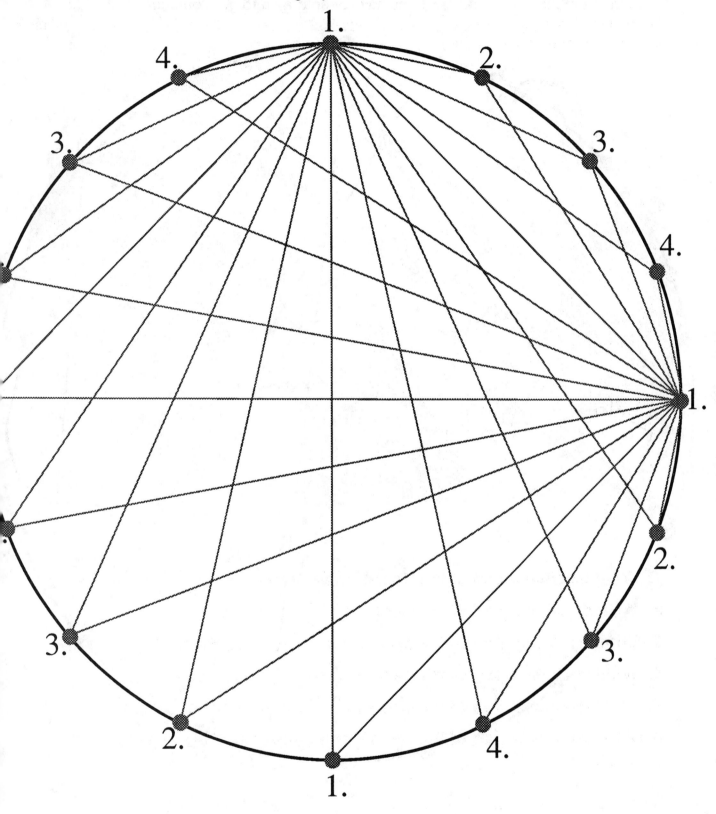

Name _____

GA1170

Line Design #2

Use a ruler to connect every point marked with the number 1 with every point marked with the number 4. The first few lines have been drawn to get you started.

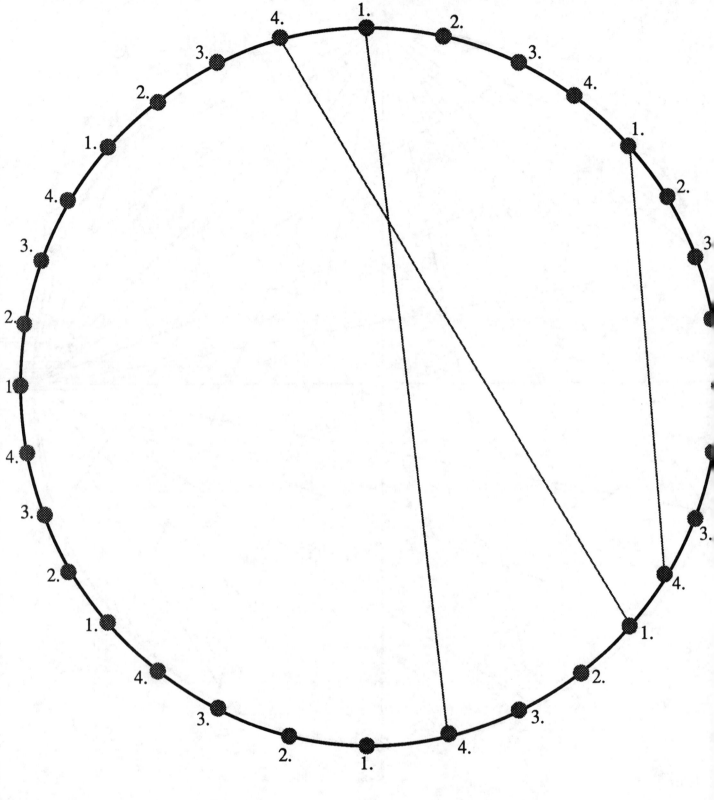

Name _____

52

GA1

It Makes Cents

1 penny = 1¢

1 nickel = 5¢

1 dime = 10¢

1 quarter = 25¢

1 half-dollar = 50¢

1 dollar =100¢

1. How many pennies equal a nickel? _____

2. How many dimes equal a half-dollar? _____

3. How many quarters equal a half-dollar? _____

4. How many pennies equal a quarter? _____

5. How many pennies equal a dollar? _____

6. How many nickels equal a quarter? _____

7. How many pennies equal a dime? _____

8. How many quarters equal a dollar? _____

9. How many dimes equal a dollar? _____

10. How many nickels equal a dollar? _____

Name _____

Bonus: How many pennies equal twenty dollars?

GA1170

Coloring Quilt #1

Each square on the quilt has a number and a letter. Example: The square in the first row and the first column is A1. The square in the second row and the second column is B2. Color each square as directed.

Red: A1,B1,I1,J1,A2,B2,I2,J2,
C3,D3,G3,H3,C4,D4,E4,F4,
G4,H4,E5,F5,C6,D6,G6,H6,
C7,D7,G7,H7,A8,B8,I8,J8,
A9,B9,I9,J9

Blue: C1,D1,G1,H1,C2,D2,G2,H2,
A3,B3,I3,J3,A4,B4,I4,J4,A6,
B6,I6,J6,A7,B7,I7,J7,C8,D8,
G8,H8,C9,D9,G9,H9

Yellow: E1,F1,E2,F2,E3,F3,A5,B5,
C5,D5,G5,H5,I5,J5,E6,F6,E7,
F7,E8,F8,E9,F9

Name _____

	A	B	C	D	E	F	G	H	I	J
1										
2										
3										
4										
5										
6										
7										
8										
9										

GA11

Coloring Quilt #2

Color each square RED, BLUE or YELLOW to create a pattern. Then write the directions for coloring your pattern. Example: If you color the square in the first row and first column RED, you will put A1 after the word *red*.

Red:

Blue:

Yellow:

Name _____

GA1170

Coloring Quilt #3

Color each square one or two times as directed. Example: The first red square to be colored is A1. That means the square in the first column and the first row. B2 is the square in the second column and the second row, etc.

Red: A1,B2,C3,D4,E5,F6,G7,H8,I9, J10,K11,L12,A12,B11,C10,D9, E8,F7,G6,H5,I4,J3,K2,L1,E3, C5,H3,J5,C8,E10,J8,H10

Yellow: A1,B1,C1,D1,E1,F1,G1,H1, I1,J1,K1,L1,A2,B2,C2,D2,E2, F2,G2,H2,I2,J2,K2,L2,A3,B3, K3,L3,A4,B4,K4,L4,A5,B5,K5,L5, A8,B8,K8,L8,A9,B9,K9,L9,A10, B10,K10,L10,A11,B11,C11,D11, E11,F11,G11,H11,I11,J11,K11, L11,A12,B12,C12,D12,E12,F12, G12,H12,I12,J12,K12,L12

Blue: F1,F2,F3,F4,F5,F6,F7,F8,F9, F10,F11,F12,G1,G2,G3,G4,G5, G6,G7,G8,G9,G10,G11,G12, A6,B6,C6,D6,E6,F6,G6,H6, I6,J6,K6,L6,A7,B7,C7,D7, E7,F7,G7,H7,I7,J7,K7,L7, C4,E4,H4,J4,D3,D5,I3,I5, D8,D10,I8,I10,C9,E9,H9,J9

Name _____

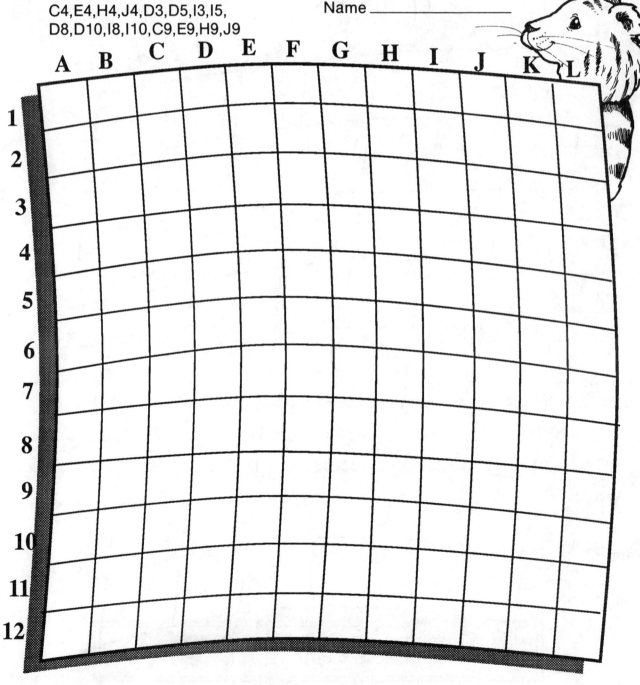

GA1

Get in Shape!

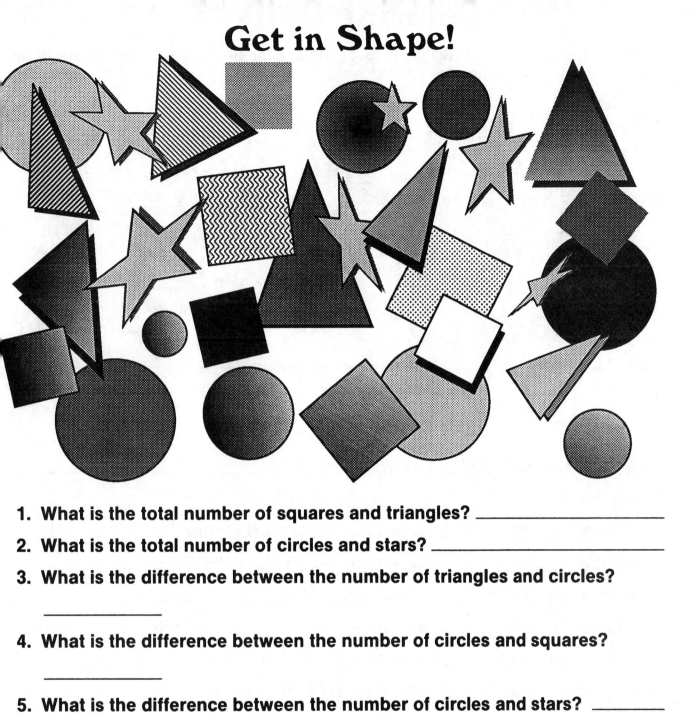

1. What is the total number of squares and triangles? _____

2. What is the total number of circles and stars? _____

3. What is the difference between the number of triangles and circles?

   _____

4. What is the difference between the number of circles and squares?

   _____

5. What is the difference between the number of circles and stars? _____

6. What is the product of squares and triangles? _____

7. What is the total of stars, circles and triangles? _____

8. What is the total number of all the shapes? _____

Name _____

Bonus: Which is greater, the product of stars and circles or the product of squares and triangles?

GA1170

Number Tank

Use the six digits in the box to answer the questions below.

1. **What is the total of the two largest digits?** _____

2. **What is the total of the two smallest digits?** _____

3. **What is the difference between the two largest digits?** _____

4. **What is the difference between the two smallest digits?** _____

5. **What is the total of the odd digits?** _____

6. **What is the difference between the two largest even digits?** _____

7. **What is the product of the two smallest odd digits?** _____

8. **What is the product of the two largest even digits?** _____

Name _____

Bonus: What is the total of all the digits in the box?

GA11

Seeing Stars!

Count the number of stars inside the different shapes to answer the questions below.

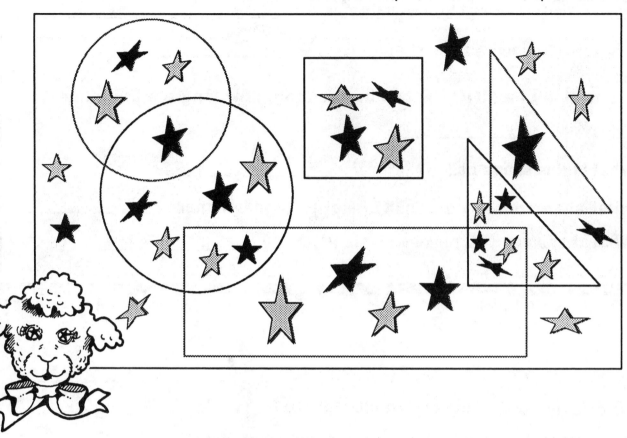

1. **How many stars are within two circles?** _____

2. **How many stars are within only one square?** _____

3. **How many stars are within two triangles?** _____

4. **How many stars are within both a triangle and a rectangle?** _____

5. **How many stars are within both a circle and a rectangle?** _____

6. **How many stars are within both a square and a rectangle?** _____

7. **How many stars are within only one triangle?** _____

8. **How many stars are within only one circle?** _____

Name _____

Bonus: What is the total number of stars that are within any two shapes at the same time?

GA1170

Mooks, Pooks and Teeks

Let's pretend that a MOOK is a shape with four equal sides, a POOK is a shape with three equal sides and a TEEK is a shape with six equal sides.

1. **What would you call this shape?** _____

2. **If one side of a MOOK is two inches long, how long are the other sides?** _____

3. **What is this shape called?** _____

4. **What shape does two POOKS shoved together make?** _____

5. **What shape can you make with six POOKS?** _____

Name _____

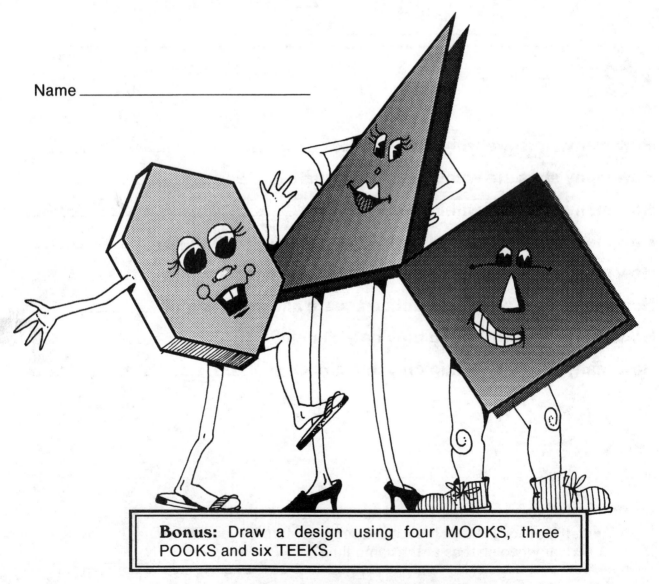

Bonus: Draw a design using four MOOKS, three POOKS and six TEEKS.

60

GA111

What Time Is It?

Use the clock below to help you answer each question.

1. **If it is 3:00, what time will it be six hours from now?** _____

2. **If it is 6:30, what time will it be two hours from now?** _____

3. **If it is 9:00, what time was it three hours ago?** _____

4. **If it is 10:00, what time will it be four hours from now?** _____

5. **If it is 12:00, what time was it eight hours ago?** _____

6. **If it is 1:00, what time was it three hours ago?** _____

7. **If it was 10:00 two hours ago, what time will it be one hour from now?**

   _____

8. **If it is noon, what time will it be in thirteen hours?** _____

Name _____

Bonus: If today is Wednesday and the time is noon, what day and time will it be twenty-six hours from now?

GA1170

Shopping for Mom

Three girls—Kathy, Karrie and Kristy—are each shopping for a present for their mother. They will buy one or more of the three presents above. Each girl has exactly two dollars. Use the price tags to answer the questions below.

1. **Kristy leaves the store with one gift and no change. What did she buy her mom?** _____

2. **Kathy bought her mom two gifts and left the store with one dollar. What did she buy her mom?** _____

3. **Karrie bought her mom two gifts and left the store with fifty cents. What did she buy her mother?** _____

4. **Which girl spent the most on her mother's gift?** _____

5. **Which girl spent half of her money on her mother's gift?** _____

6. **How much would it cost to buy all three gifts?** _____

Name _____

Bonus: How much total change did the girls have when they left the store?

GA1170

The Student Store

Use the price tags on the items above to answer each question.

1. **How much will it cost to buy two patches?** _____

2. **How much will it cost to buy three erasers?** _____

3. **How much will it cost to buy four pencils?** _____

4. **How much will it cost to buy a pennant?** _____

5. **How much will it cost to buy one of each of the four items?** _____

6. **How many pencils can you buy with one dollar?** _____

7. **How many erasers can you buy with fifty cents?** _____

8. **If you buy three pennants with a dollar bill, how much change will you receive?** _____

Name _____

Bonus: How much would it cost to buy one pennant, three patches, six pencils and four erasers?

GA1170

Apples and Bananas

Apples cost fifty cents per pound. Three large apples or five small apples equal one pound. Bananas cost seventy-five cents per pound. Three large bananas or five small bananas equal one pound.

1. **How many small apples can you buy with fifty cents?** _____

2. **How many large bananas can you buy with seventy-five cents?** _____

3. **How many small apples can you buy with one dollar?** _____

4. **How many small apples can you buy with a dime?** _____

5. **How many large bananas can you buy with a quarter?** _____

6. **How much does one small banana cost?** _____

7. **How much do three small bananas cost?** _____

8. **How many large bananas can you buy with one dollar and fifty cents?**

    _____

Name _____

Fast Food Lunch

═══ Menu ═══

Fish Sandwich $1.50

Chicken Sandwich ....45¢

Big Max $2.05

Salad $1.95

Hot Dog $1.80

Use the menu and prices above to answer each question.

1. **When Olga gave the cashier two one-dollar bills, she received a nickel in change. What did Olga order?** _____

2. **When Crystal gave the cashier a five-dollar bill, she received four bills and two coins. What did Crystal order?** _____

3. **Beth paid for her lunch with two bills and one coin. What did she order?** _____

4. **Rick paid for his lunch with two one-dollar bills and received two dimes change. What did Rick order?** _____

5. **John paid for his lunch with one bill and one coin. What did he order?** _____

6. **Who spent the most on his/her lunch?** _____

7. **Did Olga or Rick spend the most for lunch?** _____

8. **Who could have bought lunch with six quarters?** _____

Bonus: What was the total bill for the five children's lunches?

A Christmas Graph

To discover the shape of the secret picture, use the graph paper on the next page. The letter and number together give a point on the graph. The letters represent the horizontal lines. The numbers represent the vertical lines. Begin by finding point B,7. Place a small dot at this point. Next find point B,8 and place a small dot at this point. Using a ruler, draw a straight line connecting the two points. Then find the third point. Repeat until you have connected all the points. After you draw the secret shape, use crayons to color and decorate it.

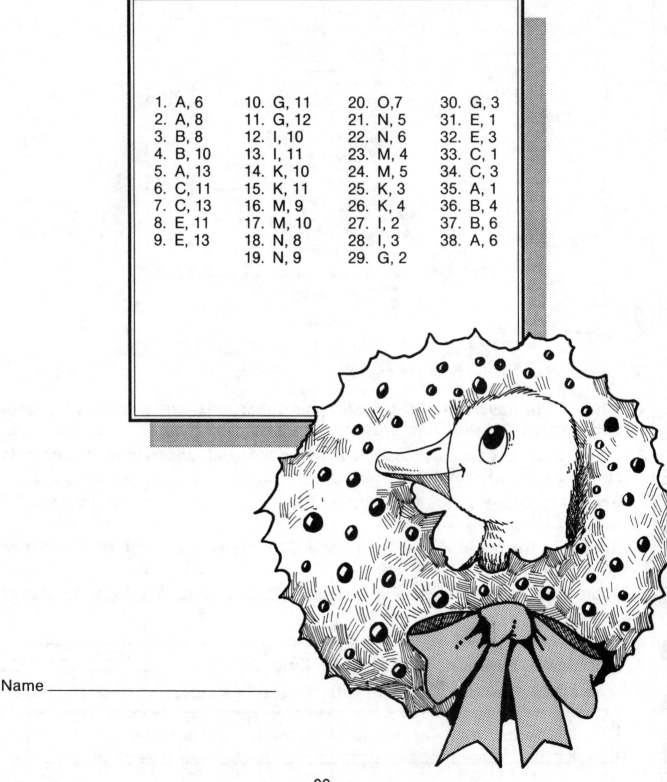

1. A, 6	10. G, 11	20. O,7	30. G, 3
2. A, 8	11. G, 12	21. N, 5	31. E, 1
3. B, 8	12. I, 10	22. N, 6	32. E, 3
4. B, 10	13. I, 11	23. M, 4	33. C, 1
5. A, 13	14. K, 10	24. M, 5	34. C, 3
6. C, 11	15. K, 11	25. K, 3	35. A, 1
7. C, 13	16. M, 9	26. K, 4	36. B, 4
8. E, 11	17. M, 10	27. I, 2	37. B, 6
9. E, 13	18. N, 8	28. I, 3	38. A, 6
	19. N, 9	29. G, 2	

Name _____

GA1170

A Christmas Graph

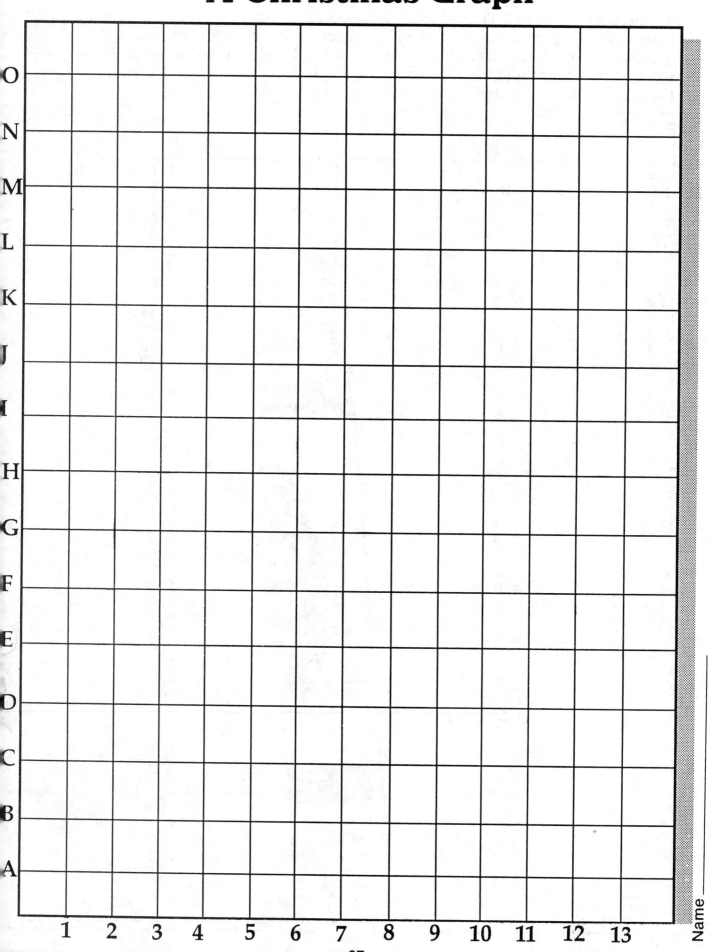

GA1170

Block Coloring

To discover the secret picture, color the squares on the graph paper on the following page. You will need blue, red and white crayons. The letter and number together give a space on the graph. The letters represent the horizontal spaces and the numbers represent the vertical spaces. To begin, color BLUE the space G,1. Continue following the coloring directions until every space has been colored.

Blue	Red		White	
G, 1	C, 2	G, 9	B, 7	B, 5
I, 2	M, 6	C, 6	L, 6	J, 10
K, 4	K, 6	I, 11	J, 6	F, 10
L, 5	I, 6	A, 3	H, 6	B, 11
L, 3	G, 6	A, 10	B, 8	
K, 5	E, 1	C, 11	L, 7	
J, 1	E, 10	E, 7	F, 1	
I, 1	C, 1	K, 11	D, 1	
H, 2	A, 5	C, 7	D, 2	
G, 5	K, 9	A, 7	J, 11	
M, 1	M, 9		B, 9	
K, 1	E, 4		H, 11	
G, 3	I, 10		D, 11	
M, 5	A, 4		H, 10	
J, 4	M, 11		D, 10	
G, 4	K, 10		L, 9	
H, 5	C, 3		F, 3	
J, 3	C, 8		F, 2	
M, 2	A, 1		L, 10	
L, 1	A, 6		J, 7	
J, 2	A, 9		B, 2	
I, 3	A, 11		J, 9	
I, 5	E, 11		H, 7	
H, 1	I, 7		F, 4	
M, 3	C, 4		D, 4	
L, 2	C, 9		D, 9	
L, 4	M, 7		B, 6	
K, 3	A, 2		L, 8	
H, 4	A, 8		D, 3	
M, 4	K, 7		J, 8	
K, 2	E, 2		H, 8	
J, 5	G, 10		F, 5	
I, 4	G, 11		F, 6	
H, 3	E, 9		D, 5	
G, 2	E, 8		F, 8	
	C, 10		D, 8	
	I, 8		F, 9	
	C, 5		B, 1	
	G, 7		B, 4	
	E, 3		B, 10	
	K, 8		B, 3	
	M, 8		F, 11	
	G, 8		H, 9	
	I, 9		F, 7	
	E, 5		D, 7	
	M, 10		L, 11	
	E, 6		D, 6	

Name _____

GA117

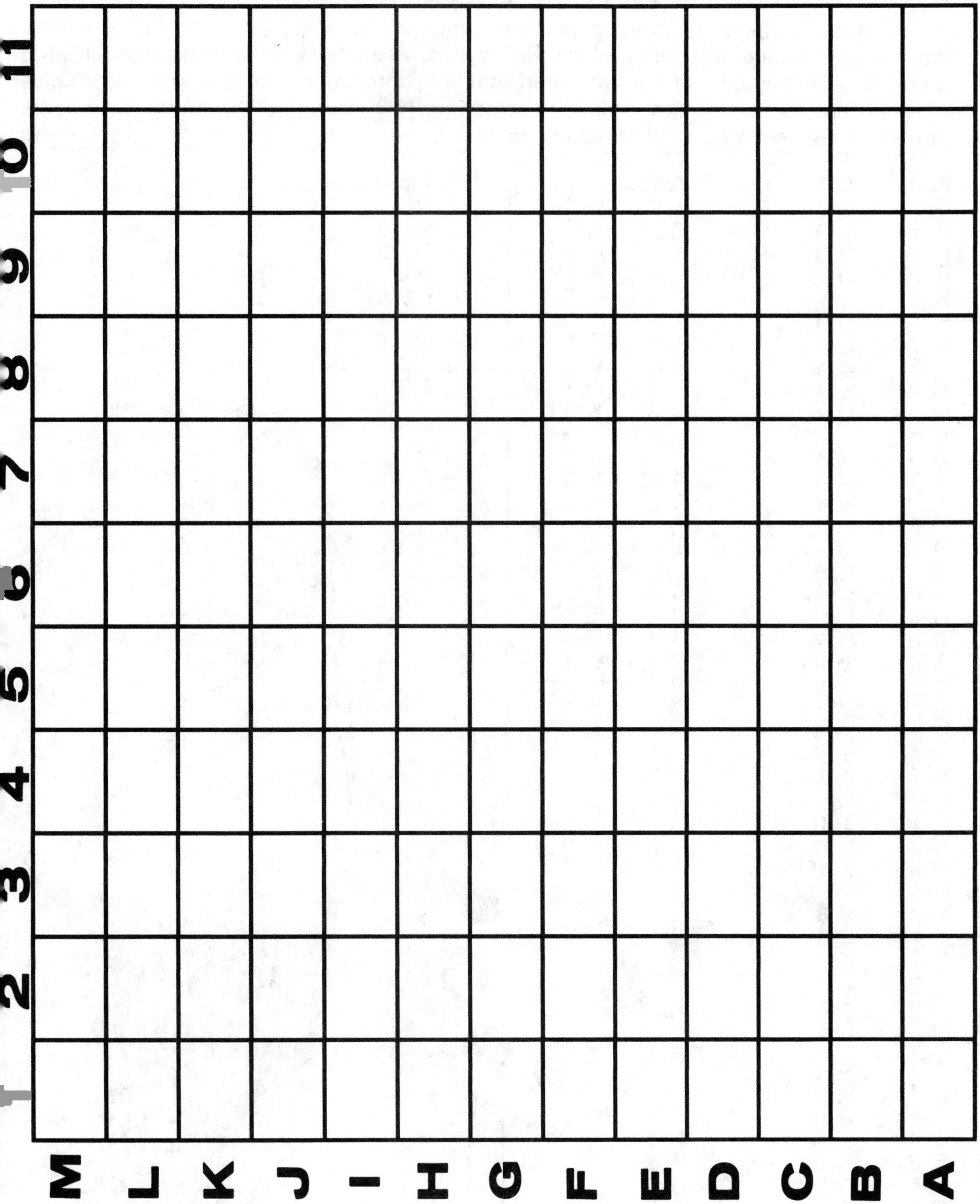
11
10
9
8
7
6
5
4
3
2
1
M L K J I H G F E D C B A

Name ______________________

Color Coordinates

To discover the secret picture, color the squares on the graph paper on the following page. You will need blue, red and yellow crayons. The letter and number together give a space on the graph. The letters represent the horizontal spaces and the numbers represent the vertical spaces. To begin, color Q,1 RED. Continue following the coloring directions until every space has been colored.

Red	A, 11	D, 6	**Yellow**	G, 7	**Blue**
Q, 1	E, 6	D, 8	B, 9	O, 10	N, 2
P, 1	M, 7	C, 1	P, 2	L, 5	M, 2
L, 1	N, 8	A, 3	P, 3	K, 6	D, 10
L, 10	Q, 2	A, 8	P, 4	F, 5	N, 3
K, 2	P, 11		P, 5	O, 9	I, 6
K, 3	O, 1		P, 6	P, 10	N, 10
N, 1	L, 2		P, 7	O, 2	M, 10
Q, 9	Q, 10		P, 8	L, 8	E, 2
M, 4	K, 10		P, 9	O, 8	E, 3
M, 5	N, 11		O, 3	K, 8	M, 3
A, 6	L, 11		L, 6	I, 8	D, 9
Q, 4	M, 6		K, 7	B, 4	D, 3
N, 6	M, 1		B, 10	H, 8	E, 10
I, 1	N, 4		C, 2	B, 3	D, 2
H, 5	Q, 3		F, 4	G, 4	E, 9
Q, 8	O, 11		J, 4	G, 8	N, 9
N, 7	N, 5		I, 4	F, 7	M, 9
J, 11	K, 11		G, 5	F, 8	
H, 6	I, 2		O, 5	K, 5	
Q, 5	Q, 7		H, 4	G, 6	
J, 2	M, 11		C, 4	C, 3	
J, 5	J, 1		O, 7	O, 6	
J, 9	H, 7		L, 7		
I, 3	Q, 6		C, 5		
I, 5	J, 3		K, 4		
I, 10	J, 6		C, 6		
H, 10	Q, 11		J, 8		
G, 2	J, 10		F, 6		
G, 3	I, 11				
G, 10	F, 10				
F, 2	M, 8				
F, 9	L, 3				
F, 11	L, 9				
E, 1	K, 1				
E, 5	K, 9				
D, 4	J, 7				
D, 7	I, 7				
A, 5	I, 9				
A, 1	H, 1				
B, 11	H, 2		C, 7		
A, 4	H, 3		C, 8		
B, 1	H, 9		B, 5		
E, 8	H, 11		B, 6		
E, 11	G, 1		C, 9		
D, 1	G, 9		C, 10		
D, 11	G, 11		B, 2		
C, 11	F, 1		B, 7		
A, 2	F, 3		B, 8		
A, 7	E, 4		O, 4		
A, 9	E, 7		L, 4		
A, 10	D, 5				

Name _____

	1	2	3	4	5	6	7	8	9	10	11
Q											
O											
N											
M											
K											
P											
G											
D											
B											
A											

GA1170

Answer Key

Guesstamation Page 1
78

More Guesstamation Page 2
1. 39
2. 27
3. 13
4. 58
Bonus: 137

Go Ahead, Take a Guess Page 3
Answers will vary.

The Price Is Right Page 4
1. 37¢   4. 25¢
2. 90¢   5. 26¢
3. 53¢   6. 42¢
Bonus: $2.73

Number Scavenger Hunt Page 5
Answers will vary.

Favorite Color Graph Page 6
1. 8   4. green, yellow, purple
2. 5   5. 3/8
3. blue   6. 5/8

The Eyes Have It! Page 7
Graphs will vary.

Flight Graph Page 8
Graphs will vary.

Pie Graph Page 9
Graphs will vary.

Using Your Pie Graph Page 10
Answers will vary.

Picture That! Page 11
1. a   4. b, no
2. c   5. b
3. a   6. c,d, 4
Bonus: About 1/2

Circle Designs Page 12
1. a,e   5. e
2. b   6. a,e
3. d   7. b,c,d
4. a
Bonus: b

Building Shapes Page 13
1. a,b or a,d   4. b,c or c,d
2. a,c   5. b,d
3. b,c or c,d

Study the Shapes Page 14
1. c   4. b, d
2. b,c,d 5. b
3. c   6. a,b,d
Bonus: triangle, square, rectangle, diamond

Two Are Out! Page 15

Bonus:

Circle One! Page 16
1. c   5. c
2. b   6. c
3. d   7. d
4. b
Bonus: a,c

Twin Designs Page 17
1. B,E   5. A,D
2. D,E   6. C,E
3. C,E   7. B,E
4. A,B
Bonus: A,C

Cross Out! Page 18
Answers may vary.
1. A (four sides)
2. C (doesn't have a circle within)
3. C (horizontal lines within)
4. A (not a square)
5. D (all other lines became progressively larger or smaller)
6. D (doesn't have repeated shape within)
7. E (doesn't have an arrow within)
Bonus: C

What's Next? Page 19
1. B (design within circle adds a line each time)
2. C (lines are vertical, horizontal, vertical, horizontal)
3. A (design is of six lines, five lines, four lines, etc.)
4. B (design adds a box within each time)
5. A (pattern is reverse the last shape: circle within triangle, triangle within circle. Diamond within square, the next shape will be square within a diamond.)
6. B (add a new V shape each time)
Bonus:

Draw What's Next Page 20
Answers will vary.

Just the Right Size Page 24
(In any order.)
1. 12: big yellow circle, big red circle, big blue circle, big red triangle, big yellow triangle, big blue triangle, big red square, big yellow square, big blue square, big red rectangle, big yellow rectangle, big blue rectangle
2. 12: small yellow circle, small red circle, small blue circle, small red triangle, small yellow triangle, small blue triangle, small red square, small yellow square, small blue square, small red rectangle, small yellow rectangle, small blue rectangle
Bonus: 1/2, 1/2

Color, Please! Page 25
1. 7: big red circle, small red triangle, big red triangle, small red rectangle, big red rectangle, small red square, big red square
2. 7: small blue circle, big blue rectangle, small blue rectangle, big blue square, small blue square, big blue triangle, small blue triangle
Bonus: 1/3, 1/3, 1/3

Shape Up! Page 26
1. 5: big red square, small red square, big blue square, big yellow square, small yellow square
2. 5: small red circle, big blue circle, small blue circle, big yellow circle, small yellow circle
3. 5: big blue triangle, big red triangle, small red triangle, big yellow triangle, small yellow triangle
Bonus: 1/4,1/4,1/4,1/4

Common Attribute Page 27
1. size   4. shape
2. size   5. size
3. color   6. shape
Bonus: Answers will vary.

GA117

Counting Attributes Page 28
2: shape, color   4. 2: size, color
1: shape   5. 0
3: size, color, shape   6. 2: color, shape
Bonus: Answers will vary.

Same the Way Page 29
shape   4. color
size   5. size
size   6. shape
Bonus: Must be same shape, size and color.

You Decide Page 30
different   4. same
different   5. different
same   6. different
Bonus: Answers will vary.

Geograms Set I Page 31

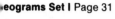

Geogram Design #1 Page 32

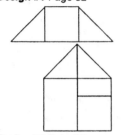

onus:

Geogram Design #2 Page 33

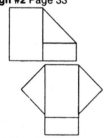

onus:

Geograms Set II Page 34

Geogram Design #3 Page 35

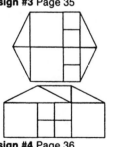

onus:

Geogram Design #4 Page 36

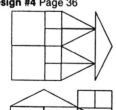

nus:

Lakeview Home Page 37
Answers will vary, should be approximately the answers found below.
1. approximately 700 yards   4. approximately 600 yards
2. Eric, Sarah and Amy   5. approximately 500 yards
3. approximately 700 yards
Bonus: approximately 1100 yards

Hidden Lunch Money Page 38
1. under the rug   4. under work table
2. in the closet   5. top drawer of chest
3. on page 50 of last book on shelf
Bonus: Answers will vary.

Dry Caves Island Page 39
1. approximately 3-4 miles
2. approximately 3-4 miles
3. approximately 6-7 miles
4. approximately 3 miles
5. approximately 3-4 miles
6. approximately 2-3 miles
Bonus: Answers will vary.

Treasure Island Page 40
Treasure is hidden under the fish-shaped rock.

Just Add a Plus Sign Page 41
1. $32 + 1 = 33$ 6. $67 + 2 = 69$
2. $4 + 50 = 54$ 7. $78 + 2 = 80$
3. $12 + 3 = 15$ 8. $45 + 1 = 46$
4. $4 + 67 = 71$ 9. $2 + 90 = 92$
5. $92 + 1 = 93$ 10. $80 + 0 = 80$
Bonus: $5 + 42 = 47$

Plus or Minus? Page 42
1. $12 + 34 = 46$ 5. $444 - 4 = 440$
2. $33 - 33 = 0$ 6. $22 + 22 = 44$
3. $111 - 1 = 110$ 7. $43 + 21 = 64$
4. $555 + 5 = 560$ 8. $98 - 76 = 22$
Bonus: $666 + 6 = 672$

Two Intersecting Sets Page 43
1. C   4. yes, 1
2. 1   5. 6
3. Mrs. Lamb   6. 3
Bonus: 2/6 or 1/3

Three Intersecting Sets Page 44
1. E   4. A
2. F   5. B
3. ice cream and candy   6. A,B,D,E
Bonus: Answers will vary.

Optical Illusions Page 45
1. same   3. same
2. same   4. same
Bonus: Pictures will vary.

More Optical Illusions Page 46
1. straight   3. same
2. same   4. b is longer.
Bonus: Pictures will vary.

Fruit Slices Page 47
1. 1/3   4. 1/4
2. 2/4 or 1/2   5. more
3. 3/5   6. 1/3
Bonus: 1/12

Easy as Pie Page 48
1. 1/4   4. 3/6 or 1/2
2. 1/5   5. 3
3. 1/6   6. 2
Bonus: lemon

GA1170

The Bobcats Page 49
1. 3/9 or 1/3   4. 4/9
2. 4/9   5. 2/9
3. 1/9   6. 0/9

Fraction Party Page 50
1. 3/10   4. 3/10
2. 4/10 or 2/5   5. 2/10 or 1/5
3. 6/10 or 3/5   6. 2/10 or 1/5
Bonus: 2/8 or 1/4

It Makes Cents Page 53
1. 5   6. 5
2. 5   7. 10
3. 2   8. 4
4. 25   9. 10
5. 100   10. 20
Bonus: 2000

Coloring Quilt #1 Page 54

	A	B	C	D	E	F	G	H	I	J
1.	R	R	B	B	Y	Y	B	B	R	R
2.	R	R	B	B	Y	Y	B	B	R	R
3.	B	B	R	R	Y	Y	R	R	B	B
4.	B	B	R	R	R	R	R	R	B	B
5.	Y	Y	Y	Y	R	R	Y	Y	Y	Y
6.	B	B	R	R	Y	Y	R	R	B	B
7.	B	B	R	R	Y	Y	R	R	B	B
8.	R	R	B	B	Y	Y	B	B	R	R
9.	R	R	B	B	Y	Y	B	B	R	R

Coloring Quilt #2 Page 55
Patterns will vary.

Coloring Quilt #3 Page 56

	A	B	C	D	E	F	G	H	I	J	K	L
1	O	Y	Y	Y	Y	G	G	Y	Y	Y	Y	O
2.	Y	O	Y	Y	Y	G	G	Y	Y	Y	O	Y
3.	Y	Y	R	B	R	B	B	R	B	R	Y	Y
4.	Y	Y	B	R	B	B	B	B	R	B	Y	Y
5.	Y	Y	R	B	R	B	B	R	B	R	Y	Y
6.	B	B	B	B	B	P	P	B	B	B	B	B
7.	B	B	B	B	B	P	P	B	B	B	B	B
8.	Y	Y	R	B	R	B	B	R	B	R	Y	Y
9.	Y	Y	B	R	B	B	B	B	R	B	Y	Y
10.	Y	Y	R	B	R	B	B	R	B	R	Y	Y
11.	Y	O	Y	Y	Y	G	G	Y	Y	Y	O	Y
12.	O	Y	Y	Y	Y	G	G	Y	Y	Y	Y	O

Get in Shape! Page 57
1. 15   5. 3
2. 15   6. 56
3. 2   7. 22
4. 1   8. 30
Bonus: 9 × 6 = 54, 8 × 7 = 56
Product of squares and triangles is greater than the product of stars and circles.

Number Tank Page 58
1. 17   5. 15
2. 5   6. 2
3. 1   7. 5
4. 3   8. 48
Bonus: 33

Seeing Stars! Page 59
1. 1   5. 2
2. 4   6. 0
3. 1   7. 3
4. 3   8. 7
Bonus: 7

Mooks, Pooks and Teeks Page 60
1. pook   4. mook
2. 2 inches each   5. teek
3. teek

What Time Is It? Page 61
1. 9:00   5. 4:00
2. 8:30   6. 10:00
3. 6:00   7. 1:00
4. 2:00   8. 1:00 a.m.
Bonus: Thursday, 2:00 p.m.

Shopping for Mom Page 62
1. silk roses   4. Kristy
2. 2 pens   5. Kathy
3. pen and card   6. $3.50
Bonus: $1.50

The Student Store Page 63
1. $1.00   5. $1.05
2. $.30   6. 10
3. $.40   7. 5
4. $.35   8. None, you'll need $.05 more.
Bonus: $2.85

Apples and Bananas Page 64
1. 5   5. 1
2. 3   6. $.15
3. 10   7. $.45
4. 1   8. 6
Bonus: $5.00

Fast Food Lunch Page 65
1. salad   5. fish sandwich
2. chicken sandwich 6. Beth
3. Big Max   7. Olga
4. hot dog   8. John
Bonus: $7.75

A Christmas Graph Page 67
Shape is a Christmas tree.

Block Coloring Page 69
Design is an American flag.

GA1

Congratulations!

You're a real

BRAINSTORMER!!!

To _____

From _____

75

HEY, BONUSBUSTER, YOU'RE GREAT!

TO

FROM

FOR

M709-IN
97

GA111